Frances Cashel Hoey, Albert Robida

Yester-Year

Ten centuries of toilette

Frances Cashel Hoey, Albert Robida

Yester-Year
Ten centuries of toilette

ISBN/EAN: 9783744754538

Printed in Europe, USA, Canada, Australia, Japan

Cover: Foto ©ninafisch / pixelio.de

More available books at **www.hansebooks.com**

TOILETTE DE BAL, RESTAURATION.

"YESTER-YEAR"

TEN CENTURIES OF TOILETTE

FROM THE FRENCH

OF

A. ROBIDA

By MRS. CASHEL HOEY

Illustrated by the Author

LONDON
SAMPSON LOW, MARSTON & COMPANY, LIMITED
St. Dunstan's House
FETTER LANE, FLEET STREET, E.C.
1892

RICHARD CLAY & SONS, LIMITED,
LONDON & BUNGAY.

CONTENTS.

I.

AN OLD SONG OF OLD FASHIONS ... *p.* 1

II.

MILLINERS' BOXES IN OLD TIMES.

Revivals—The time-piece of Fashion—Rummaging the milliners' boxes of the past—Which is the prettiest fashion?—Fashion and Architecture—Precious stones and stuffs—A dressed doll the mediæval Fashion-plate ... ... *page* 5

III.

THE MIDDLE AGES.

The painted and tatooed Gauls—The first corsets and the first false-plaits—The first sumptuary edicts—Byzantine influence—'Bliauds,' surcoats, and 'cottes hardies'—Pictorial and emblazoned gowns—The ordinances of Philip the Fair—'Hennins' and 'Escoffions'—The Crusade of Brother Thomas Connecte against the 'hennin'—The 'Lady of Beauty' ... ... *page* 24

IV.

THE RENAISSANCE.

The Fashion as to width—Hocheplis, and farthingales—La belle Ferronnière—Fans and Muffs—The gloomy fashions of the 'Reform'—Queen Catharine's 'Flying Squadron'—Laces and guipures—The stages of the farthingale—The mask and the nose-cover—Paints and cosmetics ... ... *page* 56

V.

HENRY THE THIRD.

The court of the Woman-King—Large ruffs, pleated, goffered, or in 'horns'—Bell-women—Large sleeves—Dreadful doings of the corset—Queen Margot and her fair-haired pages ... *page* 81

VI.

HENRY THE FOURTH AND LOUIS THE THIRTEENTH.

A return to comparative simplicity—Women-towers—Tall head-dresses—The excommunication of bare necks—Gowns with large flower-patterns—High necks and low necks—Long waists—Richelieu's edicts—The obedient lady—Short waists *page* 97

VII.

UNDER THE SUN-KING.

Under the Sun-King—From La Vallière to Maintenon—Gowns called 'transparent'—The triumph of Lace—The Romance of Fashion—Steinkirks—The Fontanges head-dress—The reign of Madame de Maintenon, or thirty-five years of moroseness *p.* 119

VIII.

THE EIGHTEENTH CENTURY.

The Regency—Follies and frivolities—Cythera at Paris—The Watteau fashions—'Flying' gowns—The birth of the panier—Criardes—'Considerations' and the Maîtres des Requêtes—Mme. de Pompadour—The Fan—The Promenade de Longchamps—Coaches and Chairs—Winter fashions ... ... *page* 139

IX.

EIGHTEENTH CENTURY—LOUIS XVI.

Enormous head-dresses—The pouf 'au sentiment'—Parks, kitchen-gardens, and landscapes with figures, worn on the head—The 'Belle-Poule' head-dress—Patches—Country fashions—'Negligent' gowns—Fashionable colours—Riding-habits—English fashions—The bourgeoises ... ... *page* 159

X.

THE REVOLUTION AND THE EMPIRE.

Fashions called 'à la Bastille'—Fashions of the Revolution—Notre-Dame de Thermidor—'Incroyables' and 'Merveilleuses'—Antiquity in Paris—'Athenian' and 'Roman' women—A pound of clothes—Transparent tunics—Tights, bracelets, and buskins—The reticule or ridicule—'The Victims' Ball—Blonde wigs and dog's ears—'À la Titus'—'Robes-fourreau'—Little caps and Hats—Shakos—Turbans ... ... *page* 189

XI.

THE RESTORATION AND THE JULY MONARCHY.

Full sleeves, and Leg-of-mutton sleeves—Collerettes—'Giraffe' fashions—Hair-dressing and big hats—1830—Expansion of 'Romantic' fashions—The last caps—1840—Chaste bands—Medium (Juste-milieu) fashions ... ... *page* 220

XII.

THE MODERN EPOCH.

1848—Revolutions everywhere, except in the kingdom of Fashion—Universal reign of crinoline—Cashmere shawls—The Talma, the burnous, and the 'pinch-waist' (pince-taille)—Sea-side fashions—Short gowns—The 'jump-in' costume (saute-en-barque)—Wide and narrow skirts—Clinging fashions—Poufs and bustles—Valois fashions—More erudition than imagination—A 'fin-de-siècle' fashion in demand
page 243

LIST OF FULL-PAGE ILLUSTRATIONS.

Ball-dress: Restoration		*Frontispiece.*
A Noble Lady—End of 14th Century	To face	p. 16
Figured gown and houppelande, 15th Century	,,	32
Châtelaine: Middle of 15th Century	,,	40
A Lady in the time of Charles VIII.	,,	48
At the Court of the Chevalier King	,,	56
Under Henry II.	,,	64
A Lady of the time of Charles IX.	,,	72
Court-dress under Henry III.	,,	80
Full-dress, Medicis Style	,,	88
Lady: Louis XIII.	,,	96
End of Reign of Louis XIII.	,,	112
At the Court of the Sun-King	,,	120
Under the Great King—End of 17th Century	,,	128

Under the Regency	*To face p.*	136
Court-dress: Louis XV.	,,	144
Parisienne under Louis XV.	,,	152
Large Paniers: Louis XVI.	,,	160
Parisian Ladies in 1789.	,,	168
Parisian Walking-Dresses, 1790	,,	176
'Merveilleuse' in a Greek Tunic	,,	192
'Merveilleuse' of the Directory period	,,	200
First Empire	,,	208
Parisian Lady in 1810	,,	216
Parisienne of 1814	,,	224
Stylish woman in the Champs Elysées—Restoration	,,	232
Home Toilettes, 1830	,,	240
Parisian Lady, 1835	,,	248
Seaside Fashions in 1864	,,	256

YESTER-YEAR.

I.

AN OLD SONG OF OLD FASHIONS.[1]

FROM our mother Eve's invention
  Of the very first farthingale
To Fashion's last intention,
  'Tis a dream-like passing tale.

[1] For the original verses see the Appendix.

Brief is each mode's existence,
    But Beauty is always here;
Its change is still persistence,
    Through dead modes of 'yester-year.'

Where is the gold emblazoned gown
    Bavaria's she-wolf wore;
Head-tire[1] withholding her tresses' flow,
Fought for with many a sturdy blow,
And the towering hennin, fatal crown
    That Buridan knelt before?
Forgotten, antiquated gear,
Are the dead modes of 'yester-year.'

The ruff that embattled fair Margot's throat,
    Her surcoat of ermine hoar?
The gigot sleeves, and the cavalier coat,
    Which princess and dancer wore?
Gone with the Pompadour petticoat,
Even the crinoline's graceless gear
Is dead with the modes of 'yester-year.'

[1] Escoffion.

AN OLD SONG OF OLD FASHIONS.

Envoi.

I' faith, each week had its fashions,
   From Eve's to the days that are here ;
But where are those passing passions,
   The dead modes of 'yester-year'?

The Empress Joséphine's dress-maker.

II.

MILLINERS' BOXES IN OLD TIMES.

Revivals—The time-piece of Fashion—Rummaging the milliners' boxes of the past—Which is the prettiest fashion?—Fashion and Architecture—Precious stones and stuffs—A dressed doll the mediæval Fashion-plate.

"THERE is nothing new in this world but that which has grown old *enough*," was said, not by a great philosopher, but by a woman, and she was dressmaker to Joséphine de Beauharnais, wife of Napoléon Bonaparte, Chief Consul of the French Republic, who was of her way of thinking, seeing that he resuscitated the Empire of Rome.

Acting upon this axiom, Joséphine's dressmaker tried back into the far past, even to the days of the Greek and Roman ladies, for elegant novelties two thousand years old, which were destined to turn the heads of Parisian salons and promenades, to fascinate Parisians of both sexes, and afterwards to make the 'grand tour' of the world, just as the bayonets and standards of the French soldiery, who were the most travelled of tourists, did at the same period.

You ask, Where are the modes of yester-year? said a paradoxical philosopher (he must be a married man, and harassed by dressmakers' bills), replying to my "Old song of Old Fashions," written after the method of François Villon. "You actually ask this question? Why, my dear sir, those fashions are on the backs of the women of to-day, just as they will be upon the backs of the women of to-morrow and the day after! Do you not know that nothing changes, that every novelty was invented long ago, about the time when women first began to dress themselves, within the space of four seasons, in short in the first twelve months after the turn out from Eden. I made precisely the same remark to my wife only yesterday, à propos of three or four costumes that had struck her, forsooth, by their novelty, and which she was about to order, although she did not require them. Everything is worn, has been worn, or will be worn, I told her, therefore why try to change, why lay aside for a mere whim a costume or an ornament that will inevitably 'come in' again?"

"Yes, but in three hundred years."

"My dear fellow, just go to the Champs-Elysées on a sunny day, and tell me whether you do not see visions of the Court of the Valois, when you observe some of the toilettes, with their Renaissance puffed sleeves, their

Renaissance collars, their Renaissance pictorial stuffs. Or whether you do not dream dreams of Longchamps in 1810, with those Empire gowns about, with their puffed shoulders, skirt-draping, palm-patterns, and Greek trimmings; and then the Louis Seize style, or the Mediæval, or the Louis Quinze! Why, my dear sir, a woman of any epoch whatsoever in time past, no matter how far back in the darkness of the ages, might return, appear among our contemporaries, and be quite in the fashion with only a little modification of her antique costume. Let Agnes Sorel or Margaret of Burgundy deign to reappear in the dress of their respective periods, I should merely change their head-gear, and everybody would say, "What a charming toilette for Varnishing-Day," or "What a lovely costume for the Grand Prix."

"Stay! stay! are you not exaggerating a little?"

"Not at all. I assure you the Merovingians, or even the ladies of the Stone Age, with a few little toilette arrangements to help them, would not take the women of the present day aback; they would simply be regarded as fashionable oddities. The present fashions are merely the fashions of by-gone days resumed, and recast

16th Century.

by the taste of the passing hour. The index of Fashion continuously revolves, like the hands of a clock, within the same circle, but it is more capricious, it goes now forward, now backward, with sudden jumps from one side to the other.

What o'clock is it by the timepiece of fashion? Six in the morning or eight in the evening, perhaps every hour of the twenty-four all at once, as it is at this moment. But that does not matter, it is always a charming time of day.

There is no manner of doubt, and everybody is agreed upon the point, that the present fashion is invariably the prettiest, and for the very simple reason that old fashions are only faded recollections, no sooner have they ceased to be new than their defects and absurdities become evident to our cold, severe eyes, which were indulgent during their brief reign, and the mode of the moment wins easily. What we all see in that mode, my dear sir, what charms and fascinates everybody, is the radiance of feminine grace, in fact is the woman herself! No, no, we were never better dressed than we are this very day! In all ages, and on behalf of every fashion, each woman has said this identical thing to herself and her looking-glass with perfect sincerity, and all the men have thought the same.

Our ancestress of the Stone Age, clad in skins of beasts, regarded her costume as very becoming, and smiled at the notion of her grandmother in the petticoat of a savage. The fierce cavemen, her contemporaries, were of her way of thinking.

Yes, the prettiest fashion is to-day's, the only persons who have ever denied the truth of this unvarying assertion are gentlemen 'of a certain age,' indeed of a very certain age, for these veterans, to be found at every period, have invariably passed their sixth decade. Likewise they have always entered their protest by making another assertion.

"The fashions of the day are ridiculous," they exclaim in chorus, " people don't dress as they did in our time." Then it is—in 1830, or in 1730, in 1630, in 1530 etc., even in the year 30 itself, the fashions were becoming, elegant, distinguished, charming. Ah 1830, or 1730, 1630, 1530, or the year 30! what a grand period that was!

And so we have this dinned into our ears by

the chorus of sexagenarians. Oh yes, a grand period, because it was 'the golden prime,' when these gentlemen were young, when the sun shone more brightly, the fields wore a fresher green, and the fashions were far more elegant. But all this is of no consequence, no matter what these elderly persons may say, and what we ourselves may say some years hence, the following axiom will always be proclaimed—

"We were never better dressed than we are this very day."

Since, however, nothing passes away altogether, and the lost hours marked upon the face of fashion's timepiece may all come back with the capricious circling of its hands, it is tolerably safe to predict the modes of to-morrow by merely studying those of yesterday.

Let us then rummage that vanished past, and allow ourselves the pleasure—it has some melancholy in it too—of evoking the beautiful and elegant dead fashions, buried under ages of accumulated inventions, the novelties long thrown aside and forgotten, and also the recent but no less forgotten finery of the grandmothers of the present day, who, as they recline in their easy-chairs, recall the images of themselves as

Full-dress: 15th century.

fair or dark beauties, sprightly and gay, in the attire of their spring-time. Dear old grannies!

That past which seems to us so very distant, is it really so? The grandmothers of our grandmothers were born under Louis Quinze, in the days of powder and furbelows.

Seven or eight grandmothers 'added up'—if we may venture upon such a proceeding—bring us to the time of Agnes Sorel and the tall 'hennin' head-dress. It was only yesterday, you see.

One point to be settled, to begin with, is that the art of dress and the art of construction are very nearly related. Fashion and architecture are sisters, but fashion is probably the elder.

A house is a garment; it is raiment in stone or in wood which we put on over our vesture of linen, wool, velvet, or silk, for our better protection against weather; it is a second garb which must mould itself to the shape of the first, unless indeed it be the first that adapts itself to the necessities of the second.

Without going back beyond the deluge, we may ask, Are not the pictorial, and emblazoned gowns, the cut-out, snipped-up costumes of the

Middle Ages, Gothic architecture of the most flamboyant kind, just as the more rude and simple fashions of the preceding period belong to the rude and severe Roman style?

When stone is cut, and twisted, and made almost to flash into magnificent sculptured efflorescence, the more supple textile fabric is cut and twisted and made to effloresce also. The tall head-dresses which we call extravagant are the tapering tops of the turrets which rise from everywhere towards the sky. Everything is many-coloured, the people of those days loved bright tints, the whole gamut of the yellows, reds, and greens is employed.

At a later date, costume, simultaneously with architecture, let itself out more freely. The Renaissance had come with its ampler and less rigid fashions; novelty was sought in the old. Italy acted upon dress as she acted upon building; everything, even to the princes' panoply of war or state, and the iron 'harness' of the rich nobles, was made in the antique forms, and covered with ornaments of Roman design.

The severity, indeed we may call it the gloom, of the fashions at the end of the sixteenth century, was also a characteristic of the edifices of a troubled epoch.

The ponderously wearisome and sumptuous palace of Versailles, the big dull hôtels whose

Renaissance.

architecture embodies morose conceit, are entirely appropriate coverings for the enormous and solemn wigs of the great King, and the starched tight-laced bodices and stiff 'heads' of Madame de Maintenon.

After the tedious end of the seventeenth century comes the eighteenth; the pompous

NOBLE DAME, FIN DU XIVe SIÈCLE.

and the solemn are discarded at the same time by both dress and architecture, 'rococo' toilettes, and furbelowed buildings—it is all one.

At a later date, when the people of the

Under the Great King.

Revolutionary Period and the First Empire arrayed themselves in Greek and Roman fashion, public buildings and houses did the same. From 1840 to 1860, a period of transition and expectation, both fashions and buildings were absolutely commonplace, and destitute of any style whatsoever.

Lastly, in our own time, a period of archæological research and general rummage, of experiments and reconstitution, a period of imitation rather than imagination and creation, we again observe architecture and fashion keeping step, groping together in the clothes-chests of the past, trying-on all styles, one after another, falling in love with each period in succession, and adopting its forms only to throw them aside immediately. Let us then do as our time does, let us too ransack the clothes-chests of the past in our search for the pretty things and the oddities of long long ago.

Beyond a certain period authentic documents are scarce, and we have to be satisfied with suppositions. Who shall tell us truly what were the costumes, the fashions, and the general aspect of life as presented by them, in the Merovingian and Carlovingian days, when—

> Four harness'd oxen, heavy-hoofed and slow,
> Through Paris dragged the King, a lazy show.[1]

Who shall depict for us the finery of those obscure periods? Finery there was, in spite of their rudeness and barbarism, for we find the old chroniclers in their writings already denouncing the unbounded extravagance of women.

Who shall paint for us the ladies of the time of Charlemagne, and instruct us in the modish ways of the tenth century? The few statues which have come down to us, more or less mutilated, constitute our only documents; we must content ourselves with them, and with the vague indications contained in the rude illustrations of the manuscripts of that period, so much earlier than the superb illuminations with which the artists of the Middle Ages enriched the world in a later day.

Our first Fashion-plate, then, will be some cathedral door, or statue from a tomb, that has

---

[1] Quatre bœufs attelés, d'un pas tranquille et lent,
  Promenaient dans Paris le monarque indolent.

miraculously escaped the ravages of time and the hammer of the iconoclasts, whether of 'the Religion' or the Revolution.

Under Louis Quinze.

At a later period, miniatures, painted windows, and tapestries, will furnish us with more complete and certain information, and far more precise figures; 'documents' will abound.

Besides, in the fourteenth century the actual fashion-plate existed. It had not adopted the 'gazette' shape (that has been in use for a hundred years only), but it was a journal of fashion nevertheless. Instruction in the mode travelled, under the form of dolls wearing model costumes, from one country to another, especially from Paris.

Paris already held the sceptre, and ruled over fashion, although not as she now rules from pole to pole, from the frozen shores of America to Australia—where bits of bone passed through the nasal cartilage were the only homage paid to vanity little more than fifty years ago—from the courts of the Rajahs of India to the seraglio of the Grand Turk, and the palace of Her Majesty the Empress of the Flowery Land.

In the middle ages, certain great ladies of our dear little corner of Europe, used to present each other with small dolls, dressed in the latest fashion by 'cutters,' dressmakers and tailors whose names have not come down to posterity.

Thus, on great occasions, the duchess in her distant château on the Breton 'Landes,' or the Margravine perched upon her rock on the Rhine border, would learn more or less rapidly what was the latest feat of fashion in great centres of luxury and elegance, such as the Court of Paris or the Court of Burgundy. These were rivals in novelty and display, as we learn from the accounts of expenditure that have been brought to light, with the details of the sumptuous doings which dazzled contemporaries, and are recorded by all the chroniclers of the time.

Certain important towns also received the decrees of fashion by similar means. For centuries, Venice, another centre of the sumptuary arts, and a connecting link between Eastern commerce and Western luxury, annually imported a Parisian doll. It was of immemorial custom to exhibit the waxen image of a Parisian lady, attired in the last fashion, on Ascension Day, under the arcades of the 'Merceria,' at the end of the Piazza of St. Mark, as "the toilette of the year," for the edification of the noble Venetian dames who eagerly flocked to the show.

Under Louis XII.

Escoffion.

III.

THE MIDDLE AGES.

The painted and tatooed Gauls—The first corsets and the first false-plaits—The first sumptuary edicts—Byzantine influence—'Bliauds,' surcoats, and 'cottes hardies'—Pictorial and emblazoned gowns—The ordinances of Philip the Fair—'Hennins' and 'Escoffions'—The Crusade of Brother Thomas Connecte against the 'hennin'—The 'Lady of Beauty.'

It must be boldly acknowledged that two thousand years ago, in this very Paris, which bears the standard of elegance, and triumphantly flaunts it everywhere, the predecessors of our Parisian ladies walked in the vast dark forest that stretched from the banks of the Seine to those of the Oise, and along the borders of the Ardennes, in one vast and tangled "Bois de Boulogne," clothed in a style which closely resembles that of the Maori belles of to-day.

Those rough and handsome Gaulish dames were daubed with paint, and probably tatooed; at all events, that they dyed their hair is certain.

The ornaments which have been discovered, fibulæ, torques, necklaces, bracelets, clasps in bronze and occasionally in silver or gold, afford evidence that those primitive semi-savages were accustomed to a certain kind of luxury. There is a great analogy between their style of ornamentation, and that which prevails in Brittany at the present day.

Ancient Gaul, Gaul of the Barbarians, having become Roman Gaul, the Gaulish women, in imitation of the Roman, speedily exhibited a taste for all the refinements of civilization and luxury. Ladies! the corset dates from their time, but it was a corslet of thick stuff which moulded the form, rather than an instrument of torture which distorted its lines.

The primitive love of vivid colouring did not decline at once; but actual paint became merely rougeing, and essences for preserving the complexion, and also false plaits, had already been invented. These locks, of a reddish-fair hue—the same colour has been in fashion for a long time past—were purchased from German peasant girls, the Gretchens of the time of Arminius.

The invasions of the Franks were followed by a return to barbarism and simplicity; their women, who were big and strong, knew of no greater luxury in dress than a chemise striped with purple.

Little by little, the Roman fashions, mingled with the Gaulish, the Frankish, and the

Merovingian fashions, of which a few stiff and hieratic statues give us a notion, underwent a transformation.

The great Emperor Charlemagne, he of the flowing beard, in the midst of his Court, where the wives of his dukes and counts indulged the most unbridled taste for adornment, sumptuous stuffs and jewellery, observed a strict simplicity of attire for himself, as Frederick the Great and Napoleon did also. He was shocked by the growth of display and extravagance, and he was the author of the first sumptuary laws, which were naturally observed only by the bourgeoises; those good ladies did not require prohibitions to deprive themselves of finery which they could not purchase for lack of money.

We may contemplate the people of those days in effigy in the tall hieratic figures sculptured under the porches of our most ancient churches. Rows of kings and queens, stiff and stern, set-in beneath the old archways, princes and princesses lying on raised stone

slabs, old spectres of rudely carved stone, who
shall tell us whom these really were, and what
was that living and moving world over which
they presided?

They keep their secret, it is hidden behind
the mysterious brows of those sculptured
phantoms, standing in the entrances of the
buildings which they founded, or lying in the
museums to which they have been con-
signed.

Our cities—trodden by the descendants of
those ancestors, graceful French women, who
crowd around the brilliant shops of the present
day in which life is so intense—our own old
cities were in existence then, but how often
has their aspect changed! Every vestige of
those times has disappeared, their last stones
are buried under the foundations of the oldest
buildings now standing.

We know almost as little of the ways of life
at that period as we know of village civilization
in the dolmen era, and we have to search in
the earliest and most ancient poems or romances

of chivalry, amid the clash of lance and battle-axe, for a few traces of its social history.

We come to the Middle Ages, when the

Surcoat with Garde-corps.

Byzantine influence of Rome, transplanted to the Bosphorus, at first prevailed in the clothing of both men and women, and was supreme about the time of the earliest Crusade. This was the period of long gowns with very close folds, of double girdles, one worn at the waist and one round the hips, and of transparent veils. It was in reality an age of transition. Fashion was groping about, turning backward, and resuming forgotten forms with certain

Ceremonial head-dress, 14th century.

alterations; the Roman costume, modified at first by Byzantium, rearranged and semi-orientalized, was partly restored.

Then suddenly, at the dawn of the thirteenth century, when a new era was emerging from the twilight of ancient barbarism, the new fashions declared themselves, frankly and plainly.

This was the actual birth of French fashion, of costume purely French, like the ogival art in architecture that sprang from our soil, and discarded all that was imitated, or borrowed, in short every reminder of Rome and Byzantium.

The statuary, the stained glass, and the tapestry of the Middle Ages, will now supply us with the very best of documents. Those figures carved in full dress upon their tombs, an actual resuscitation of the noble châtelaines of the period, are extremely remarkable portraits, with all the details of attire, the garments, and the head-dress clearly indicated, and in some instances still bearing traces of painting which give us the colours of the costume.

The stained glass is still more interesting, for it represents all classes of society, from the noble lady to the woman of the people; in memorial windows, in the windows of seigneurial chapels, or the chapels of city corporations, in the great compositions with portraits of the donors beneath the storied windows, the noble dames in rich attire kneeling opposite to the good knights in armour, the rich 'city madams' opposite to the worthy aldermen or 'notables' their spouses.

Tapestries are not entirely trustworthy as veritable records, for the artist sometimes introduces decorative fancies into his compositions; nevertheless, we find many figures in them which afford precise indications, corroborate the testimony of the statuary and the glass, and may be added to the innumerable and marvellous illustrations of the manuscripts of the time.

Above the under-dress, the petticoat, or 'cotta,' the women of the eleventh century wore the 'bliaud' or 'bliaut,' an ornamented robe of fine stuff, held in to the figure by a girdle. The 'bliaud,' which was at first made of merely goffered stuff, was soon enriched with designs and ornaments in very good style.

The transformations of the 'bliaud' and the 'cotta' are endless. The under-dress became the

ROBE ET HOUPPELANDE HISTORIÉES XVᵉ SIÈCLE.

'cotte hardie,' and the 'bliaud' was supplanted by the surcoat. This under-dress, which fitted very tightly, was laced in front and at the back, and showed the outlines and shape of the body.

In the full-dress costume a 'garde-corps,' or bodice-front of fur, was added to the surcoat and lent it additional richness. The general form, however, was subject to a number of particular arrangements, cottas and surcoats varied in all manner of ways, following the fashion of the day, the taste of individuals, and the mode in the provinces, or in the small princely or ducal courts, which were isolated by circumstances or situation.

How superb they were, those belles of the Middle Ages, with their long clinging gowns, covered with regularly repeated designs of rose-form, and alternate squares of different colours, making a kind of chessboard of the whole body, or flowers and foliage in large groups, frequently woven in gold or silver. These stuffs took grand folds, and draped themselves naturally in statuesque lines; from samples

D

of them which still exist in museums, we may judge of the effect they must have produced when made up into stately trailing gowns.

A noble Châtelaine.

Armorial bearings, which came into existence with the earliest social organizations, with the first heads of clans or warrior-chiefs, but were regulated at a later period, appeared upon the ladies' gowns, which were stamped like their husbands' shields with symmetrically arranged escutcheons.

This custom found favour, the fashion 'took,' as we should now say, and very soon heraldic designs were displayed more fully upon the gowns called 'cottes historiées.'

Let us summon up a vision of these noble dames at Court, or on festive occasions in their castles, in those vast halls now open to all the winds that blow, and inhabited only by crows, —always the last dwellers amid feudal ruins— let us fancy them seated at the tables of state, between the lofty fire-places and the musicians' gallery, or else on the platforms or 'eschaffaux' alongside of the lists stricken for the famous tournaments. There they are, arrayed in robes emblazoned through all their length with the arms of their husbands or their families, displaying, like living standards, every invention of the heraldic art, portraying all the beasts of its menagerie, lions and leopards, wyverns and griffins, wolves and stags, swans and crows, sirens and dragons, fishes and unicorns, all of them of fantastic aspect, all winged, nailed, clawed, horned, and toothed, issuant, passant, and rampant on glittering fields, gules, vert, and azure.

And the non-heraldic robes, strewn with great curving flowers, or highly-decorative designs, are not less rich or less brilliant.

The shapes of the period, although they seem to be very various, are all on the same principle. The surcoat has no sleeves, it is opened more or less widely at the side from the shoulder to the hip, in order to show the under-dress which is of another colour, but harmonizes with the upper, and is either more or less covered with designs than the surcoat, so that there should not be equality in this ornamentation.

A 'garde-corps' or bodice-front of ermine adorns the upper part of the surcoat; the fur is cut low on the shoulder to exhibit the bosom, which was very liberally uncovered, especially in full dress. A band of ermine bordered the cut-out portion of the surcoat on the shoulders and hips.

There was great variety in the shapes of the bodices, both of surcoats and cottas, in shoulder ornaments, and in the methods of baring the neck. Certain modes were immodest; preachers denounced against the immorality of fashion from the pulpit, and the reciters of the old 'fabliaux,' who are not prudish, made fun of them.

Upon the invention of linen cloth, women were not satisfied with baring their necks in order to show their linen gorgets, or the tops of their chemises, they devised the plan of cutting their gowns open at the side, leaving long apertures from the shoulder to the hip, laced across and exhibiting the linen underneath.

At that time, as at every other, certain fine ladies persisted in exaggerating the vagaries of fashion. Some of these fair dames wore gowns so narrow and so clinging that they seemed to be sewn up in them, or else the surcoats were so much too long that the superfluous material had to be tucked into front pockets in which the hands also were placed, otherwise the skirt was gathered up and

The little Hennin.

fastened to the girdle. The latter alternative was a very pretty fashion, and formed those delightful broken folds which we see in the drapery of statues.

The sleeves of these long surcoats, with the

'serpent-tail' train, which great ladies were allowed to have carried by a page, became elongated also. The sleeves of the under-dress came down to the wrist with an outward slope which covered a portion of the hand. The wider sleeves of the surcoat were either open from the shoulder, and hung down almost to the ground, or slit from the elbow to the wrist, or made with only an aperture through which the fore-arm passed.

There were several varieties in sleeves, long, wide, or tight; sleeves cut and buttoned underneath from shoulder to wrist, sleeves cut out, or puffed at the elbow, even the sleeves called 'à mitons' were worn, the end forming close mittens, and 'pocket-sleeves' closed at the ends; these were pretty and convenient inventions after all.

Lastly, there were vast sleeves like wings, with edges cut like the teeth of a saw, or like oak leaves, or bordered with a thin line of fur.

Jewellery assumed great importance. All

women, whether great ladies or bourgeoises, adorned their costumes with jewels of greater or less price; necklaces, head-circlets ornamented with precious stones placed upon the head-piece, jewelled buckles, and girdles of wrought braid and gold work.

The 'aumônière' or 'escarcelle' (literally, alms-bag) attached to the girdle was made of rich stuff bordered with gold, with a gilded clasp and ornaments. The great ladies were dazzling, they literally shone. The sumptuary laws were quite ineffective. In vain did Philip the Fair enact and ordain, forbid ermine and miniver to the bourgeoises, and debar them from golden girdles set with pearls and precious stones, in vain did he decree that:—

"No damoiselle, if she be not châtelaine or dame owning 2,000 livres yearly shall have more than one pair of gowns per year, and if she be, she shall have two pairs and no more.

"In like manner also the dukes, counts, and barons owning 6,000 livres yearly shall be

CHATELAINE, MILIEU DU XVᵉ SIÈCLE.

allowed to have made for them four pairs of gowns per year, and not more, and for their wives as many . . ."

In vain did Philip the Fair fix a maximum price per ell on stuff for outer garments on a descending scale for all sorts and conditions of people, from twenty-five sols the ell for barons and their wives, down to seven sols for their squires, and—a remarkable testimony to the wealth of the townspeople and shopkeepers of the great cities even in that bygone time— permit the wives of the bourgeois to go so far as sixteen sols the ell; in vain did he provide against everything, and make stringent rules; nothing availed, not even the threat of fines. Great ladies and wealthy city dames alike defied the commands of the king, the remonstrances of their husbands, and the admonitions lavished upon them from innumerable pulpits.

In vain did the preachers attack every part of the costumes in vogue, denouncing the occasionally indecorous slits in the surcoat as 'doors of hell,' the shoes 'à la poulaine' (so-called after the spur of a ship) as 'An outrage on the Creator,' and waging a bitter war against the head-dresses, whether 'cornettes,' 'hennins,' or the high head-tires called 'escoffions'; the

The Hennin with large veil.

women simply let them talk, and imperturbably followed the fashions.

In matters of the Mode, women were then, as they are now, a law unto themselves, they ignored all authority, royal, ecclesiastical, or marital.

The ladies of the period wore shoes 'à poulaine'; those famous shoes with their turned-up points were adopted by the other sex, and adorned with a little ringing bell at the curved end.

High heels were as yet unknown, but they gradually grew out of a kind of slipper with several soles placed one above the other. Head-dresses assumed extravagant proportions, and the 'Hennin' triumphed over all its rivals. The 'Escoffion' took various forms, now that of a crescent, anon that of a turban; then there was the heart-shaped cap, a pompous head-tire of embroidered stuff, trellised with braid, adorned with beads, and having a wide frontlet set with jewels, which came down to the forehead in the form of a heart. It was, however, the great horned 'escoffion' that gave offence in particular to the preachers; this curious structure consisted of a broad cylinder of rich stuff ornamented with jewels, terminating in two horns, with a streamer of fine muslin which fell upon the shoulders from each point.

These 'escoffions'—(the term is obsolete, and has no equivalent in English)—were said to come from England, like many other eccentricities of costume at all times. The Anglomania that breaks out now and again, dates from afar. Viollet-le-Duc gives an example in his *Dictionnaire du Mobilier* of a 'grand escoffion' on the statue of a Countess of Arundel who lived at the beginning of the fifteenth century. Preachers and moralists, comparing the women who wore those head-dresses to horned beasts, and to pictures of Satan, declared that she who had been unfaithful to her husband twelve times would go to Purgatory, but they cast directly and immediately into Hell the wearer of a horned escoffion.

The 'great hennin' was a tall conic tube in brocaded stuff worked with beads, and tightly fixed upon the forehead. It closely confined the hair, and had a short veil in front, but from the top of the towering edifice a cloud of fine muslin floated and fell around the figure. It was an unreasonable and inconvenient structure, it is true, but it was not ridiculous, it was monumental, but charming, and women persisted in wearing it for nearly a century, because it was in reality very becoming, and imparted an imposing effect to the countenance and to the entire figure. There was another reason also for this feminine persistency, which was probably not taken into account, but only unconsciously recognized; it was that these 'great hennins' harmonized with the architecture of the age.

What a magnificent epoch of expansion and elevation was that! The church-spires, slender and darting upwards, scaled the sky and drew men's souls upward with them, all the lines of architecture sprang upward, spread out, and blossomed into richness. When we reflect that this was the time of marvellous façades of houses or palaces, of slim turrets, and of scalloped roof ridges, the time when the towns bristled with innumerable spires and clock-towers, it is easy to understand the tapering height of the hennin. Like all ascensions it also was a rising towards the ideal, for the lofty head-tire with its long floating veil gave nobility to the attitude and gait of the wearer.

Nevertheless, the cry of the monks and the preachers was "War to the hennins!" The most urgent of them all, and the most widely-heard, if not listened to, was a Carmelite monk of Rennes, named Brother Thomas Connecte. He undertook a regular campaign in his own town against the prevalent extravagance, and in particular against the poor hennins. From Brittany he proceeded to Anjou, Normandy, Île-de-France, Flanders, and Champagne, preaching ardently everywhere, and discoursing in the cities from a lofty platform erected in the open air in the most public place, overwhelming the women who took delight in the refinements of dress with invectives, and threatening them with the Divine wrath.

All the misfortunes that were falling upon

the world, all the vices of the time, all the sin, shame, and turpitude of humanity, came,

The great Hennin.

according to Brother Thomas, from the culpable extravagance of the hennin, and the satanic escoffion. In the ardour of his conviction the good friar did not stop at words; he seized a staff at the end of his sermon, burning with pious zeal, and pushing through the frightened crowd of women of all classes who had come to hear him, he effected a pitiless massacre of hennins, in spite of loud cries and vigorous hustling.

"Down with the hennin! Down with the hennin!" now became the cry of the idlers and vagabonds, stirred up by Brother Thomas, as they hunted any woman whose head-dress exceeded the modest proportions of an ordinary coif through the streets.

For all that, sermons and molestation notwithstanding, the hennins were none the worse, but rose up as tall as ever after the monk had gone on his way. From town to town the latter continued his crusade, until at length he reached Rome, and there the unedifying spectacle presented by the capital of Christendom at that time excited him to such a pitch that he passed all bounds, and letting the hennins alone, he attacked the

DAME SOUS CHARLES VIII.

princes of the Church. This was a more dangerous game, and the poor man, being accused of heresy, was arrested and burned in public.

The history of Fashion has the romance of fashion in it also! What curious episodes there are in the annals of feminine coquetry, and what romantic figures appear in them, some figures full of witchery and charm, some strangely poetical, but also occasionally dangerous syrens, witnesses against his age on behalf of poor Brother Thomas Connecte.

The history of Fashion might be written with a dozen portraits of women spread over the centuries; portraits of queens of the right hand and queens of the left hand—more frequently the latter—great ladies and great courtesans. We need only name them; with each name we turn a page, or begin a new chapter: Agnes Sorel, Diane de Poitiers, Queen Margot, and Gabrielle d'Estrées, the first wife and the last 'mie' of Henri Quatre, Marion Delorme, 'la grande Mademoiselle,'

E

Montespan, in the first period of the Sun-King's reign, Maintenon in the second period, that of the soured and world-worn monarch,

Cut out and pinked sleeves.

Madame de Pompadour, the triumph of the dainty eighteenth century, Marie Antoinette, the last sad ray of splendour of a world that had come to its end, Madame Tallien, Joséphine Beauharnais, &c.

The Houppelande.

After Isabeau of Bavaria, Queen of France and of the Mode, the handsome and magnificent wife of Charles VI., she who was at first the queen of balls and festivals, but soon became the queen of the civil wars, without, however, abandoning her sumptuous costumes and fastidiously elegant surroundings —after the time and fashions of Isabeau, come the time and the fashions of Agnes Sorel, the 'Dame de Beauté' of Charles VII.

Charles is idling at Bourges, no longer even thinking of reconquering his kingdom; his mistresses and his pleasures make up his world. The great and saintly Joan has put on male armour and gone forth to fight the English; she has already reconquered a large portion of his realm for the king; another woman who is neither great nor saintly is about to carry on her work. This is Agnes Soreau de Sainte Géraud, the beautiful Agnes Sorel, a blonde with blue eyes. By the power and ascendancy of her beauty she impels the King, her august servant, to attack the English, she makes him recapture the remainder of the realm of the fleur-de-lys, town after town, and earn from history the name of Charles the Victorious.

It is she who is victorious. The sinews of war are employed in paying the King's troops, and providing arms and provisions, likewise in defraying the cost of the luxurious living of the Lady of Beauty, and her innumerable whims. "These," says an old romance, "are also the expenses of war, since the king fights better when Agnes commands him."

That heroic maiden, the valiant Joan, donned her cuirass to lead dukes, lords, and men-at-arms to conflict; the fair Agnes, adored by the king, worked for the national cause after a totally different fashion; she bared her shoulders, invented bodices indecently cut down to the waist, and enlarged the great hennins with floating streamers. And the King's troops marched, taking castles, towns and provinces, and hunting out the English. Agnes may be said to have died on the field, for she expired near Jumièges during the reconquest of Normandy, whither she had followed the king.

The Court of Burgundy, which was the rival of the Court of Paris in display as well as in all other things, brought strange elements into French fashion, especially from Flanders. This importation inaugurated the last epoch in the costume of the Middle Ages, the final blaze, dazzle, and glitter of their strange and gorgeous attire.

The gigantic 'houppelande' or mantle worn by both men and women resembles a large piece of tapestry—the outlines are lost in the complication of the design. After a period of transition the Renaissance was coming.

We might dwell on many other interesting and pretty things, features in the costume and general adornment of the women of the Middle Ages, in the ceremonial attire, made of splendid stuff, and with glittering garniture, in the indoor and outdoor clothing of all classes, as well as in the travelling and hunting dress worn by noble ladies who rode richly-caparisoned mules upon their journeys, or trained palfreys on their hawking parties, and carried jessed and hooded falcons on gauntleted wrists.

Under Francis I.

IV.

THE RENAISSANCE.

The Fashion as to width—Hocheplis, and farthingales—
La belle Ferronnière—Fans and Muffs—The gloomy
fashions of the 'Reform'—Queen Catharine's 'Flying
Squadron'—Laces and guipures—The stages of the
farthingale—The mask and the nose-cover—Paints
and cosmetics.

IMMEDIATELY after the expeditions of Charles
VIII. a gust arose, and blew upon the modes
of the Middle Ages. The Gothic period had
come to an end; the costume of men was

A LA COUR DU ROI-CHEVALIER.

suddenly transformed, and that of women was about to alter in its turn. That wind carried away our national architecture and our national taste, with many other things, for instance, the hennin, which, in spite of appearances, became its wearers' heads so well that the mode had lasted for nearly a century.

Costume became less formal and more complicated. The corset or bodice superseded the surcoat; it was low-cut, not of the same colour as the gown, and was laden with ornaments and gilded designs, while necklaces of several rows of beads or jewels covered the upper part of the neck. The sleeves again were of a different colour from the bodice; and now we come to the great streaming, wing-like sleeves, with cut-out edges, and to sleeves made in several pieces fastened together by tags or ribbons, and showing the chemise of fine Friesland linen, puffed at the shoulders and elbows. This was the beginning of the sleeves with alternate puffings and slashes, which were destined to last so long.

Toed, or square-ended shoes, succeeded long-pointed shoes; for fashion always goes from one extreme to its opposite. There was great variety in head-dresses, but all were low. Turbans which covered the whole head, also coifs embroidered in gold that framed, so to speak, the forehead and the face, were much worn; these turbans and coifs, ornamented with beaded nets, were modified in countries where Flemish or Rhenish influence contended with Italian influence, by the addition of a sort of slashed hat, which grew by degrees into the wide 'béret' of the Swiss or German lance-bearers.

At this period a fashion arose which was adopted, alike by noble ladies and wealthy dames of the bourgeoisie, throughout the whole of the reign of Francis I., at the dazzling Court of the Knightly King, and also in the cities.

The chief innovation, destined to influence all the other garments, and partly to define their cut and proportions, and to be thenceforth the dominant note of costume, was the farthingale.[1] This was a thing hitherto unknown, a great novelty which upset the whole system of costume, and changed all its lines.

The farthingale, that is to say, the wide skirt supported by a contrivance of one kind or another, "came in," to stay "in" for three centuries. It lasted for three hundred years, with intervals of more or less duration under different names: panier, crinoline, pouf, tournure, bustle, dress-improver, &c. It still lasts, and we shall see it flourishing again.

For three hundred years the width of skirts runs a regular course; it increases little by little, slowly, accustoming the eye progressively to its proportions; it reaches a formidable, excessive, impossible expansion, then it de-

---

[1] Vertugadin, vertugalle, or vertugardien.

creases gradually, passing the reverse way through all its former stages.

Women, whom the farthingale has trans-

Beginning of the Renaissance.

formed for a shorter or longer period into big bells, become once more little bells, 'small by degrees, and beautifully less,' until the farthingale is supposed to have vanished.

THE RENAISSANCE

For some years very clinging garments are worn, then just an insinuation of bustle reappears, a little touch of farthingale is discernible in skirts, and the inevitable process begins once more.

The farthingale triumphs still, in spite of the unsparing abuse, the comic songs, and the increasing ridicule lavished upon it ever since its invention, and even in spite of the edicts which attempted to reduce its dimensions. No power in the world has had so many enemies arrayed against it, no institution has been so vigorously and eagerly attacked.

Monarchy and Republicanism have adversaries, but they have advocates also. The farthingale, whether as panier or crinoline, had every husband, every man against it. The corset only competes with it in the multitude of its enemies—and the corset also has invariably beaten them.

The farthingale, which came into existence under Francis I., about 1530, marks the end of the Middle Ages more clearly and completely than any political change whatsoever marks it. The clinging or hanging gown, with its straight sculptured lines, has disappeared. A world is ended.

The farthingale was at first known as the 'hocheplis,' or shake-folds. This name was applied in the first instance solely to a stiffened pad, stretched upon a wire frame, which was attached to the waist to give width to the skirts. Afterwards the name was extended to a construction of cane or whalebone, forming a cage under the petticoat.

The costume of women in the reign of Francis I. was ample and majestic rather than graceful; gowns were made of velvet, satin, and flowered brocatelle, of various colours, with wide hanging sleeves, lined with sable, or enormous puffed sleeves raised over the shoulder, and forming a succession of rolls down to the wrists, with slashes showing puffs of light silk.

The busked corset, then called 'basquine,' appeared at this period. Very probably there was a separate apparatus worn underneath the bodice, but the bodice itself was stiffened by means of whalebone; at all events, the confused descriptions of the basquine, which are all we have, lead us to think this may have been so.

Certain modes of adjusting the bodice, to which objection might well be taken, had been imported from licentious and effeminate Italy, and men also went bare-necked. Large sums were expended in jewellery and goldsmith's work, for the ornamenting of head-dresses— the 'attifet,' the 'chaperon,' and the 'toque.' Queens, noble ladies, and bourgeoises, impoverished themselves by buying gold chains, enamelled trinkets, pearls, and other gems.

La belle Ferronnière, one of the mistresses of Henri Quatre, who succeeded the Duchesse d'Etampes, invented the fashion of wearing a carbuncle hung on a gold thread, in the middle of the forehead. One more jewel to be worn, when the head-dress, the bodice, and the girdle, were already laden with sparkling stones; what a charming idea! The head-dress à la Ferronnière achieved an immediate success.

Several additions to dress, hitherto unknown, came into use at this period. For summer there was the feather-fan, a pretty pretext for goldsmith's work in the mounting; for winter there was the muff. According to the royal decree, black muffs were for the bourgeoises, coloured ones for noble ladies only. Parasols were also imported from Italy, but did not 'take' to any great extent; they were too heavy.

But now the extinguisher of 'the Reform' popped down upon the brilliant epoch of the Valois King, and a dark, troubled time set in.

Fashion, which had been brilliant, lavish, and superb in its sumptuous amplitude during the reign of Francis I., a chivalrous, prodigal, and ostentatious prince, in an age of dash

SOUS HENRI II.

and 'bravery,' and of licence also, was about to change its character suddenly, and to become as austere as it had been showy, as

Slashed sleeves.

sombre and melancholy as it had been brilliant and full of colour.

At the beginning of the reign of Henri II. there was a tough struggle between the gloomy and the gay fashions, but the former very soon beat the latter, and by degrees the bright and frivolous modes vanished, and were succeeded by dark colours, eventually indeed by plain black.

The times were troublous, and tending towards blackness too. In the train of 'the Reform,' with its religious dissensions, its wars of sermons and controversy in the first place, came actual war, waged with cannon and arquebus, stake and gallows.

In 1549, Henri II. opened hostilities against luxury in dress, by an edict interdicting a great number of ornaments and stuffs, trimmings, borders, gold lace, cloths of gold and silver, satins, &c., and strictly regulating the fashion. This edict prescribed the kind and quality, and even the colours, of the stuffs to be worn by the different classes.

The right of wearing a complete vesture, both upper and under, of crimson hue, was reserved to princes and princesses exclusively; the nobles, male and female, were permitted to display that brilliant colour in only one article of their costume.

Ladies of the next rank had the right of wearing gowns of every colour except crimson, and their inferiors might wear a dull red or black. The same sliding scale was appointed for stuffs, from satins and velvets to plain cloth. Loud cries of lamentation resounded throughout the country when the edict was about to be enforced.

The ladies of France, from north to south, from east to west, closed up their ranks, and bravely defended, inch by inch, their stuffs and their colours, their jewels and their trinketry, disputing with the agents of authority, and advancing a thousand ingenious reasons for keeping everything they had got.

The King had to resume his pen, and to complete his edict by a series of explanatory clauses, detailing point by point what was permitted and what was prohibited. He made certain concessions to the ladies, and allowed them a few little coquettish indulgences; but outside of these what was forbidden remained forbidden, and the sumptuary law was rigorously enforced.

> " Le velours, trop commun en France,
> Sous toy reprend son vieil honneur,"

says Ronsard, in a letter to the King, in which he praises the reformatory decrees of Henri II.

Catherine de Médicis, that gloomy princess, whose blood poisoned the blood of the Valois, the murderess who died full-fed upon crime, now predominated over the Court of France—it was still brilliant—like a black phantom, emblematic of the approaching era of crime and massacre.

The head-dress of Catherine de Médicis.

She left the artifices of coquetry to the Court ladies and to Diane de Poitiers, her husband's mistress, the supreme beauty, the semi-mythological goddess of the Renaissance, of whom Jean Goujon made a statue, even as Canova long afterwards sculptured Pauline Borghese, another princely beauty. The prettiest creations of the age are dark-coloured costumes, elegant but severe, composed of harmonies in gray, or harmonies in black and white, the colours of Diane de Poitiers.

Under Henri II.

At the death of Henri II., Catherine assumed the costume of a widow, and this she never laid aside. Surrounded by a swarm of brilliant young beauties, her Maids of Honour, who were called " The Queen's flying squadron "—

a squadron that served her to better purpose in her innumerable schemes than many squadrons of swash-bucklers — she passed through the three troubled reigns of the kings her sons in black from head to foot, black like the night, black like her own soul.

A wide skirt in black stuff, a black, pointed bodice, with large, black, wing-sleeves attached to the shoulders, a black collar, ruff-shaped, and for head-dress a sort of hood or toque, with a front which comes down in a point upon a brow busy with dark designs; such was her costume.

It seems that it was Catherine who imported ruffs into France, when she arrived from Florence for her marriage; and these ruffs (fraises) were adopted at once by both men and women.

Ruffs were of all sorts, moderate and outrageous, very simple ones in pleated lawn, and others in wonderful lace. The ruff was a charming invention, it had its drawbacks no doubt, like many another device of fashion, but its quaint shapes, in filmy lace, formed a dainty frame to the faces of fair women, which looked out from gems in a setting of fine workmanship.

The decorative elegance of the Renaissance was largely due to the master-pieces of the essentially feminine art of lace-making. The same artist who worked in bronze, in gold, or in silver, who carved wondrous decorations in stone on the façades of palaces, supplied the designs for ruffs; lace had its Benvenuto Cellini, at Brussels, at Genoa, and especially at Venice, the chief centres of lace-making.

It was not until the time of Henri III. that the ruff assumed its full proportions. At first it was merely a gorget with round stiffened folds which encircled the throat from the collar-bone to the ears, the harsh close-pleated ruff of a period of increasing gloom. Protestant austerity had been gaining ground rapidly, and although the Catholics retained their more facile manners and customs, the religious quarrel had become very bitter, and civil war brooded over France.

Under the ephemeral reign of Francis II., with its passing glimpse of poor Marie Stuart, and her aureole of fate, and under that of Charles IX., costume was of a discreet and sober fashion. Men's doublets and women's bodices were slashed, like the stiff sleeves puffed at the top. The only articles of jewellery worn were the buckles and pendants of the girdles called 'cordelières,' the mounts of the 'aumônières,' and a necklace underneath the collar, which was a small fluted ruff, with cuffs of the same material.

In 1563 Chancellor de l'Hôpital, a declared foe to extravagantly wide farthingales, had succeeded in contracting and diminishing them by a severe decree, which also interdicted the wearing of padded hose by men. But it came to pass that the King (Charles IX.) visited Toulouse, and the fair dames of that place petitioned him for a relaxation of the edicts of the stern Chancellor, whereupon the King,

DAME DU TEMPS DE CHARLES IX.

acting with greater clemency on this occasion than he afterwards did towards the Huguenots, pardoned the farthingale, and allowed it to resume its vast proportions.

We must not mock at the farthingale's circumference, for it saved France, if there be any truth in the chronicle that records how Marguerite de Valois rescued her husband Henry of Navarre from death, by hiding him under an immense farthingale, while the perpetrators of the massacre of St. Bartholomew were cutting to pieces with their halberts the unfortunate Huguenots who had been housed in the Louvre on the occasion of the wedding of the Béarnais and Margot.

The fashions became dull and sombre like the architecture and the furniture of the time, like everything indeed. This was a general law, architecture no longer displayed the overflowing luxuriance, the pagan gladness of the Renaissance, its forms became more staid. After a time of riot in the merriest inventions, architecture was doing penance. The furniture of the new and grim hôtels was stiff and clumsy. The square tables and chairs, without carving or any ornament, were made of rough wood covered with coarse stuff edged with big nails; in catafalque style.

Under Charles IX.

The dwellers in these dull buildings, in apartments which seem to be hung with funeral trappings, were at this period personages clad in sad-coloured attire. Long gowns with high bodices were worn over wide farthingales, the bust was confined and compressed in a stiff busked corset, clasped at the back, worn over a bodice which was also stiffened and whaleboned.

Out of doors women wore light pattens, with cork soles, underneath their shoes: this had been a custom of previous times, but many were the jests passed upon ladies of short stature who perched themselves upon pattens of formidable height, or increased their inches by putting several soles to their shoes.

The head-dress of the period was either the coif with a net—the pointed front making the face heart-shaped—that we now know as 'the Mary Stuart' coif, or the black-velvet hood. The latter was not becoming.

It was 'bad form' for noble ladies, and indeed for the city dames also, to go out unmasked. The strange fashion of the mask was another note of gloom added to the already prevalent depression.

Masks, made of black velvet, were short, allowing the lower part of the face to be seen, or had chin-pieces; they were fastened behind the ears, or kept on by a glass button held between the teeth, the latter was considered the more elegant method. The fashion of the mask passed on from the ladies of quality to the lower ranks of the bourgeoisie, and held its ground until the time of Louis XIII.

The mask was becoming and coquettish, not so the 'touret de nez,' a piece of black stuff attached by the sides to the hood, and fixed under the eyes, which hid all the lower part of the face. This odd invention resembled the yashmak of the Cairene women, but was more unsightly.

These nose-concealers had, it appears, a reasonable origin. Let us not lift them up. The ladies of that time painted outrageously, after a fashion which had come from Italy with Catherine de Médicis; they simply daubed themselves like Caribs, and plastered their cheeks under the 'touret de nez' with pigments which were very bad for the skin. The female face was covered with plasters of vermilion, or else, under pretext of preserving the freshness of the complexion, with ill-smelling pomades and drugs.

Horrible!

An "Instruction pour les jeunes dames"

throws a light upon the composition of these 'ointments,' or rather deplorable messes, in which turpentine, lily-roots, honey, eggs, egg-shells, camphor, etc., were mixed up, and the whole boiled in the inside of a pigeon, then mashed, and distilled together.

The 'touret de nez' seem to have been indispensable after that.

René, the Florentine who was brought to France by Catherine, and maliciously styled "The Queen's Poisoner," supplied the fair court ladies with paints, perfumes, and cosmetics, besides concocting for the Queen-Mother the more deadly medicaments which she used for— in a manner at once discreet and refined—the suppression of troublesome persons.

What a time it was! From one end of the kingdom to the other the strife of parties raged; men hated, disputed with, and fought each other.

During a period of thirty years everything was confusion, the Catholic and Huguenot armies chased each other through the provinces, each in its turn sacking the towns, burning the castles, waging a merciless war in which neither women nor children were spared, a war of ambushes and massacre.

Stuff with raised designs.

The towns were besieged, the country was ravaged by the Catholic 'argoulets' and arguebusiers, and by the Protestant 'reiters,' castles and manors were carried by assault. They who were the weaker had to fly, or to perish.

It is easy to see that in such a time as this the dress of women must necessarily assume a somewhat masculine character. In moments of peril the poor women were frequently forced to escape on horse or mule-back, sitting like men.

Condé, being surprised in an interval of peace (in 1568), and forced to fly from his castle of Noyers near Auxerre, and make for Rochelle in order to escape from Catherine's troops, was obliged to cross the Loire with his pregnant wife carried in a litter, three infants in the cradle, the families of Coligny and Andelot, and a number of children and nurses.

The women adopted a kind of doublet, with upper-hose, to be worn under the gown. These 'caleçons' (drawers), as they were called, enabled them to sit on men's saddles and use the stirrups more easily, notwithstanding their wide skirts.

In spite of everything, the farthingale flourished and increased in magnitude.

"Et les dames ne sont pas bien accommodées
Si leur vertugadin n'est large dix coudées."

We find this couplet in a satire of the period, entitled *Discours sur la mode*.

In the time of 'the Reform.'

TOILETTE DE COUR HENRI III.

The Valois head-dress and collar.

V.

HENRY THE THIRD.

The court of the Woman-King—Large ruffs, pleated, goffered or in 'horns'—Bell-women—Large sleeves—Dreadful doings of the corset—Queen Margot and her fair-haired pages.

No vital change in the situation was brought about by the reign of Henry the Third. The times were perhaps more gloomy, and the country was more disturbed. In spite of the

Holy League, however, and notwithstanding the spread of the Civil War, and the blood that was flowing everywhere, Henry the Third, king of torn and tormented France, laid his hand on the sceptre of fashion.

After the melancholy Charles, who regarded luxury in dress with disdain, came a foppish king, curled, ruffed, scented, rouged, who, while he renewed the sumptuary edicts of his late brother, led the Court, and, after the Court, all who had it in their power to follow the fashion, into every kind of luxurious folly and eccentric extravagance.

Disorder reigned at the Court of this "King of the Island of the Hermaphrodites," as the pamphleteers called him, d'Aubigné's "King-woman and man-queen."

> "Son visage de blanc et de rouge empâté,
> Son chef tout empoudré nous montrèrent l'idée
> En la place d'un roi d'une fille fardée."

"Such are the luxury and the license," says the *Chronique de l'Étoile*, "that the most chaste of Lucretias would turn into a Faustina there."

The kingdom of fashion itself was disturbed, its natural frontiers were obliterated, and the distinctions of costume for the two sexes were disregarded. The King, whose taste was singular, made his own dress as feminine as possible, seeking what he might borrow from the attire of women, from the head-dress to the fan.

Like the ladies of the Court, the King and his 'mignons' took to wearing pearl necklaces, ear-rings, Venetian lace, and large ruffs. Also like the ladies of the Court, and others, he painted his face, and used cosmetics in the most ridiculous manner, even wearing a mask and gloves steeped in pomade at night. These were strange effeminate ways for a time of unsheathed dagger and constant peril. The 'mignons' and the 'popelirots' wore a sort of corset to give them slim waists, the busked doublet, coming down low to a sharp point, speedily became the absurd doublet with a padded front forming a kind of Punch-like protuberance. The 'mignons' and 'popelirots' also adopted the feminine 'toque,' adorned with feathers and precious stones.

Women borrowed nothing from male costume, but they made up for this by considerably exaggerating the dimensions and the ornamentation of the component parts of their own, by wearing the most sumptuous stuffs, and loading themselves with jewellery.

Marguerite de Valois, the King's sister, the Queen Margot of Henri Quatre, led the fashion. In all except his absurdity, from which her feminine grace preserved her, she was a match for that astounding prince her brother, the curled, painted, and musk-scented satrap who starched and goffered his own ruffs and the Queen's, and took his walks abroad with several little dogs in his arms or a cup-and-ball in his hand.

Ruffs assumed fantastic proportions; they became immense, widened-out horns stretched on brass wire of magnificent lace or Venetian-point embroidery, which rose from the bodice, while showing the shoulders, to above the back

Court dress.

of the head, indeed to the summit of the head-dress. The painted face thus framed in sharp-edged lace was like a brilliant flower or fruit, or rather like that of an idol, over-coloured and laden with jewellery and tinsel.

The bodice was actually covered with jewels, and what with gold, gems, beads, necklaces, ear-rings, and diamonds and pearls in their head-

The Mask.

dresses, princesses and great ladies shone and twinkled all over. Head-dresses were very low, the hair was arranged in a point on the forehead and raised in rouleaus on the temples, forming the shape of a heart surrounded by a circlet set with jewels and pearls.

Rows of pearls formed square or lozenge-shaped designs on the bodices and skirts. The girdle, with very long ends, was also of jeweller's work; at one extremity hung a small mirror, richly set, which the wearer had in her hand constantly, so that she might inspect the condition of her precious but troublesome attire, and especially the immense ruff, which was a serious inconvenience, with all its majestic elegance, on social occasions, and at the crowded Court entertainments.

It is easy to estimate what the burden of the costume of the period must have been, by merely looking at a picture in the Louvre which represents a Court Ball given on the marriage of the Duc de Joyeuse with the King's sister-in-law. This was a famous wedding, celebrated with unexampled splendour by twenty-five or thirty days' festivities, jousts and masquerades, during which the entire Court, princes and princesses, lords and ladies, vied with each other in the fantastic sumptuousness of their daily-changed costumes.

According to this picture, which is attributed to Clouet, lords and ladies competed for the palm of absurdity in their costumes. It shows us nothing but pointed bodices preposterously

Padded sleeves.

tightened, and doublets with pointed abdomens, so that both men and women have the appearance of insects, the former looking like big bees, the latter like wasps.

GRANDE TOILETTE MÉDICIS.

The ridiculously long-busked bodices have enormous padded sleeves, as thick on the shoulders as the whole body, and formed of a series of rolls and slashes, edged with pearls or gilded braid, with cuffs of fine lace to match the ruff.

The farthingale had been considerably enlarged, it was now of a bell-shape, or like an enormous soup-tureen turned upside-down; over it two garments were worn, the upper-dress, of rich brocade or stuff covered with embroidery, was open so as to display the under-dress of a different colour but equally ornamented.

When the troubles and the confusion of the time were at their worst, when Leaguers, Royalists, and Huguenots were shooting and hanging each other all over the kingdom, Damville, the eldest of the Count de Montmorency's three sons, who had taken up arms for a fourth party, that of the 'politicals,' who were allied to the Huguenots in the South, became seriously indebted to the invention of the cumbersome farthingale. Being surrounded at Béziers, he was about to be taken, and in great danger, but one of his relations, Louise de Montagnard, the wife of

The short Henri Trois cloak.

Francis de Tressan, carried him off in her coach, hidden under the spreading width of her immense farthingale, and passed him through under the very nose of his enemies.

This was the second instance of salvage by the farthingale, but there may have been many more which history has not deigned to record. The crinoline, an old acquaintance of our own, has no such deeds of high emprise to its credit. Its vast circumference was indeed also utilized, not for such dramatic escapes, but by fraudulently-ingenious females, who carried articles on which they ought to have paid duty slung on its hoops.

The corset was no longer the simple 'basquine'; that was inoffensive enough at first. The 'corps piqué,' which was endured by the fair ladies of this later period, was an instrument of torture, a hard and solid mould into which the wearer had to be compressed, there to remain and suffer, in spite of the splinters of wood that "penetrated the flesh, took the skin off the waist, and made the ribs ride up one over the other." Montaigne and Ambroise Paré are witnesses on behalf of this indictment of the 'corps piqué,' and the latter, at least, must have known something about it.

Like the farthingale, 'only more so,' the corset will witness the burial of successive ages, will survive all other fashions, notwithstanding every attack upon it, and the doctors who are unanimous in their excommunication of it, and

Under Henry III.

will be ever-victorious over all and sundry, victorious against the clearest evidence. The absurd 'mignons' of Henry the Third actually succeeded in making men adopt it for a while!

HENRY THE THIRD.

The celebrated beauties of the time, Queen Margot, and her husband's mistress Madame de Sauves, look like idols braced up in damascened cuirasses, in their state costumes, with their stiff, glittering bodices, and their

Margot.

gorgeous array of gold and precious stones. "Touch me not!" say those formidable pointed ruffs, and yet the wearers of them were by no means inaccessible.

All the women of the period, sad and

sombre as it was, were bitten by this mania for luxury. There was not one of the smaller nobility, or a lawyer's wife, or a 'city madam,' who did not try to imitate the great ladies in everything, to the displeasure of their husbands,

Full dress, Médicis style.

and the peril of fortunes which had already suffered by the evils of the time.

The brilliant sixteenth century, the age of the Renaissance, which gave birth to so many artists and men of letters, to doughty knights, and dazzling dames, came nevertheless to a bad end. Over that termination, about that epoch of Henry the Third with his corrupt refinement, about the Court and the City, about fair and noble women and exquisites and 'mignons,' there hung a scent of blood which it needed all the strong perfumes, the musk and amber then in vogue, to overpower and disguise.

Marguerite de Valois, a flower whose perfume was deadly, was to survive this epoch, and to die in 1615, some years later than Henri Quatre, her former husband. To the last she was an old coquette, painted, bedizened, and musk-scented, and she strove, in despite of her age, and the corpulence that destroyed her goddess-like pretensions, to keep up the solemn and stately graces and the state costumes of her best days. She migrated regularly with her little Court from her château in Languedoc to her Parisian Hôtel de Sens, which still exists, now and again promoting to her good graces some handsome cavalier, or some pretty page—a page like those mentioned in the chronicle of her earlier years, when she was accused of having their boyish locks shorn to make light-coloured wigs for her own wear.

Shortly before the death of this princess, now "the grotesque Margot," one of these petted pages was stabbed under her roof by an equerry who aspired to the exclusive possession of the favour of the aged Queen. Marguerite became as infuriated as a wounded lioness, and in order to avenge the object of her very latest love she claimed her feudal right of doing justice in her own house (in Scottish feudal times, this was called the right of "pit and gallows"), condemned the guilty person to death, and had him beheaded forthwith under her own bloodthirsty eyes, in the presence of a mob, on the very threshold of the Hôtel de Sens.

DAME LOUIS XIII.

The collerette ruff.

VI.

HENRY THE FOURTH AND LOUIS THE THIRTEENTH.

A return to comparative simplicity—Women-towers—Tall head-dresses—The excommunication of bare necks—Gowns with large flower-patterns—High necks and low necks—Long waists—Richelieu's edicts—The obedient lady—Short waists.

SOME eras live long, but others die young; the sixteenth century, which had an exceptionally strong constitution, lasted until the end of the reign of the Béarnais, with its ideas and its manners, its ways and its modes. We shall afterwards see that the seventeenth century lasted in the same way under Louis XIV. to the detriment of the eighteenth, and that the charming but unfortunate eighteenth century came to a melancholy and premature close, dying suddenly in the year '89.

The years of grace of the sixteenth century, under the sceptre of Henri Quatre, were like convalescence after brain-fever; while they lasted, France, reduced to extremity by her malady, revived, the poison was expelled from her veins, all was repaired, cleansed, and sanitated.

After the absurd and unwholesome devices of the reign of Henry the Third, dress assumed an unpretending character, an aspect of good, honest frankness, if we may be permitted to talk of frankness in dress. The costume was, indeed, but little altered, but the lines were simplified, and all that was superfluous in the details was suppressed.

No doubt the fashions for both sexes were

less elegant, and there was a good deal that was absurd in them even yet, but this absurdity was harmless. Excessive pretension, with dissolute grace and refinement, had been discarded; but fashion, in seeking simplicity, had strayed into heaviness and awkwardness, only, however, to emerge from both into the bold and dashing elegance of the costume of the period of Louis XIII. Yet we must not take this simplicity too literally, for it was only comparative.

On occasions of state the ladies displayed just as much jewellery as before. The queen by whom the divorced Marguerite was succeeded (a second Médicis Marriage which was not much of a success for the Béarnais, who had already only too much reason to remember Catherine), Marie de Médicis, the "queen of the right hand," as the saying was, and Gabrielle d'Estrées, Duchesse de Verneuil, queen "on the side of the heart," with all the other fine ladies, appeared "at fêtes, ballets, masquerades, and collations, richly adorned and magnificently attired, and so laden with precious stones that they could not move about."

On one great occasion the queen wore a gown sown with 32,000 pearls and 3,000 diamonds, and her example was followed by lesser personages, who cheerfully expended more than their revenues in dress and its accessories, in garments of brocade, satin, and exquisite damask, flowered and bordered with gold, and laden with various kinds of jewellery. This was an odd sort of simplicity, and yet, when we examine the pictures and prints of the time, we clearly perceive that a great difference existed between the ultra-refinements of fashion in the time of Henry III. and its somewhat clumsy finery in the time of Henri IV.

Head-dresses were higher, and a great quantity of false hair, of the colours in vogue, was worn.

For a while, wigs of the Louis XIV. and Louis XV. fashion were adopted, but only by ladies; these wigs were of fair, or brown hair, or even of tow, for those who could not afford the more expensive kind. With wigs came powder, a kind of starch in which pomade was mixed with powders of various kinds, from the finest, perfumed with violet and iris, to plain flour for the use of simple country ladies.

Patches (which reappeared in the eighteenth century), also came into fashion at this time, but were at first as large as plasters, and less becoming than the coquettish 'assassines' of a later date.

The women of the people, and the smaller bourgeoisie, still wore the hood of former days, a modest head-dress, while the ladies of the upper classes, whose hair was bedecked with beads and jewels, wore hats or the plumed toque.

After so many gloomy years, people were happy to live and breathe, yet a fashionable lady was bound to be strapped up in a hard and rigid corset, strongly armed with whalebone, an actual sheath, which came down in a point upon her skirt, all of a piece, without any indication of form. It must be said, however, that the women indemnified themselves for this terrible article of attire by wearing bodices, also cut down in a point, and so liberally,

Court dress under Henri IV.

that His Holiness the Pope thought it necessary to interfere, and to threaten those who persisted in baring their necks to excess with excommunication.

This menace had no great effect, the penalty

attaching to the next world only; large ruffs, and upstanding collars of superb lace mounted on wire, continued to encircle and enhance the charms which were disclosed by the accommodating bodice. Fine lace looks so well near the skin, it throws out the shape and whiteness of the shoulders, and the shoulders show off the marvels of Venice or Flanders point, the jewel-work of the needle, to perfection.

Enormous sleeves, which were not sleeves, were attached to the bodice. These were open wings, hanging down very low from the shoulders, trimmed with closely-set buttons that did not button. The real sleeve showed beneath, was padded and raised at the shoulder, and had cuffs at the wrist called 'rebras.'

Skirts were less balloon-like than formerly, the farthingale was more moderate, it now resembled a bell, hanging straight and heavily, or rather the big drum of a Swiss battalion, but the hips were padded in cupola shape, and marked out grotesquely by a row of stiff puffings of the same stuff as the gown.

It was difficult for women clothed in such a style to have a light and graceful gait; nevertheless the ladies of the period liked those cumbrous skirts, and the ideal of elegance was to affect the waddle of a duck in walking, so as to give them a rhythmical swing.

The Fair Gabrielle.

A correctly-dressed lady wore three skirts under her gown, all of different colours, and variously trimmed. These three skirts she was supposed to show, by lifting up her gown in a skilful and elegant manner.

There was plenty of choice among the fashionable stuffs and colours, within the following series of names, as comical as those which were afterwards invented in the whimsical eighteenth century.

Sad friend colour, doe's belly, scratched face, rat colour, fading flower, dying monkey, gladsome widow, lost time, dead-alive, sick Spaniard, mortal sin, common ham, chimney-sweep, &c., &c.

The Regency of Marie de Médicis was a period of transition between the fashions of the sixteenth, and those of the seventeenth centuries; the real Louis Quinze costume did not shake off the last vestiges of the Renaissance fashions until about 1630, at the time of the reformatory edicts of Richelieu. These edicts condemned ladies to rest content with simpler stuffs and under-clothing by prohibiting cloth of gold and silver, gold lace, embroidery, trimming in gold thread, and fine laces, and so forced the tailors, who cut and made the clothes of both men and women, to invent new shapes.

During the earlier portion of this reign

fashion cast off much of its heaviness, the farthingale became beautifully less, the ugly

After Callot.

padded roll above the hips disappeared, and was succeeded by a great bunch of the drawn-up folds of the under-skirt.

The farthingale, thus snubbed in its home, crossed the frontier to reign in Spain under the name of 'guarde-infante,' and presently assumed proportions so vast, that, in order to arrest their growth, the authorities, imitating those of France, resorted to edicts. Seizure and public exhibition of the prohibited articles was added to fines, and the strict application of the decree was met by sturdy resistance, and even by tumults and bloodshed. Nevertheless, so long was the life of the farthingale on the other side of the Pyrenees, that the gallants of the court of Louis XIV. beheld it, worn by the ladies of the Spanish Court at the famous interview in the Île de la Conférence where the marriage of Louis with Marie-Thérèse was arranged.

In France, taste, richness, and display, the multiplicity of ornaments, the wearing of a quantity of jewellery, became fashionable again, and the ladies, even those of the mere bourgeoisie, indulged in a superfluity of costly clothes and trinkets.

How "a lovely woman conducts herself in dress," a satirical poet tells us.

> "Il lui faut des carcans, chaînes et bracelets,
> Diamants, aliquets et montants de collets,
> Pour charger un mulet, et voire davantage—
> Il lui faut des rabats de la sorte que celles
> Qui sont de cinq ou six villages damoiselles ;
> Cinq collets de dentelle haute de demi-pié
> L'un sur l'autre montés"—

Although farthingales were smaller, ruffs had gone on growing in height and size; the great portraits by Rubens, and afterwards those by Van Dyck have preserved the semi-circular ruff of the latest period, sweeping out behind the head.

We may derive full information concerning Parisian fashions before and after Richelieu's edicts, from the engravings of Callot and Abraham Bosse.

Callot, whose marvellous graver had designed so many gallant cavaliers in doublets of silk, or buff leather, so many officers in jackets,[1] and

[1] *Hongreline*—the word is obsolete.

noble gentlemen of the true seventeenth-century type in the smart costumes which they wore with so fine a presence and such easy grace, has also engraved some feminine costumes of the same period, but retaining the style of the previous century. Callot's ladies still wear the gowns with long waists, the stiff 'corps-piqué' corset, padded sleeves with slashes of bright colours, and skirts drawn up over the reduced farthingale. The new-fashioned shoes had flaps,[1] and were tied above the instep.

> " Les bourgeoises non plus que les dames ne vont
> Nulle part maintenant, qu'avec soulier à pont,
> Qui aye aux deux côtés une large ouverture
> Pour faire voir leurs bas, et dessus pour parure
> Un beau cordon de soie en nœud d'amour lié."

This is an accurate description of the Louis XIV. shoe, which was so smart and so elegant. There are many admirable specimens in the rich collection of the Musée de Cluny, cut low, and with black ornaments on the tan leather, and some plain ones with the ribbons

[1] *Pont-levis.*

tied in love-knots. The side openings showed rose-coloured stockings, the fashionable colour. Crimson velvet pattens, with very high soles, were worn with these shoes.

Gloves were equally elegant; they had

Médicis ruff.

patterns on the back, and arabesques embroidered on the gauntlet[1] which enclosed the wrist.

The dresses, and indeed all the stuffs of the period, were covered with bunches of

[1] *Grand crispin.*

flowers. The present Jardin des Plantes, formerly Jardin du Roi, owes its existence to this fashion; the primitive nucleus of it, in the time of Henri Quatre, was the garden

Louis Treize bodice.

of a shrewd horticulturist, who grew all sorts of French and foreign plants, with a view to supplying models to the designers of stuffs or embroideries.

Head-dresses varied. For a long time they

remained very high, so as to avoid the ends, or 'horns' of the ruffs, were waved or curled like an Astrakhan cap, and adorned with jewels only. At a later period ruffs were so altered as to be either bands of cut-lace falling on the square opening of the bodice, or low, if not actually flat, collars.

With these later ruffs it became possible to lower the head-dress; a small chignon called 'culbute' was formed behind the head, and the face was framed in pretty falling ringlets or frizzed curls. When this fashion became exaggerated, women's heads looked like round balls, with their frizzy curls and little rings of hair plastered on the forehead.

Now came the stern edicts of Richelieu, who was resolved to prevent French gold from going out of the country to enrich foreign manufacturers by the purchase of Milanese silk braids, and laces or embroideries, to the detriment of French commerce. The edicts afterwards prohibited gold lace and fringe purfling, and lace work enriched with gold

FIN DU RÈGNE DE LOUIS XIII.

and silver stripes, and gold or silver fringes, allowing only narrow stripes of simple stuff. Costume was about to change all of a sudden.

Bourgeoise of the period of Louis XIII.

"Il faut serrer ces belles jupes
Qui brillent de clinquants divers.
On a pris les dames pour dupes,
Leurs habits n' en seront point couverts,"

says a lady, drawn by Abraham Bosse in 1634, after the issuing of the edicts and the reformation of costume.

The change was radical; no more overloading with ornaments, no more flowered stuffs, no more fine lace from Brussels or Venice. The "lady according to the edict," drawn by Abraham Bosse, wears, over a flat skirt with straight-falling folds and not the slightest sign of farthingale, a bodice with basques, very high at the neck, and fastened by a plain ribbon, the wide sleeves open upon an undersleeve, without either trimming or embroidery.

The large ruff, the big frill, either high or flat, is succeeded by a band ('rabat') of lawn which comes up to the chin. In this costume there remains nothing of the fashion of the sixteenth century; that mode is dead for good and all, it is of 'yester-year.'

But the new costume, very simple and sober, almost to the point of austerity, is destined to become the fixed costume of women of lesser rank, those bourgeois house-wives, to whom sumptuary edicts cause neither care nor pain; in fact, in its outlines, it is the costume actually worn by the sisters of Saint Vincent of Paul.

Then did the fair dames take this modest costume, "according to the edict," and quickly transform it into one of the most elegant

End of the reign of Louis XIII.

and charming ever invented by fashion, a truly remarkable type of high distinction, at the very moment when the masculine costume of the earlier days of Callot, so free, and manly, and knightly, was about to change for the worse, to become heavy and constrained, with the jerkin waists up under the arms, and the upper-hose, or breeches, falling over the calf of the leg.

The gown was now worn open from the top to the bottom, showing a bodice-front of light satin, ornamented with tags, and ending in a rounded point on a skirt of silk or reddish-brown satin. The upper dress was widely divided, and rather long, all its folds were on the sides or at the back. The puffed sleeves were cut in narrow bands, fastened on the inner side of the elbow by a ribbon, or opening on a rich under-sleeve of lace, and trimmed at the aperture with tags or bows of ribbon.

No more high frills, only flat ones. The large collars and bands of lawn again displayed some rich embroidery on the points, which fell very low over the shoulders and on the arms, and pointed cuffs of the same embroidery, reaching from the wrist to the elbow, were adopted.

Bunches and tufts of ribbon everywhere, rosettes on the bodices, garlands of rosettes at the girdles, necklaces of pearls falling on the bosom, strings of jewels fitting to the

An élégante of the time of Louis XIII.

neck, diamonds and stones on tags and shoulder-knots; such was the array of the fashionable lady in 1635, who displayed her rich apparel on the Place Royale to the moustached gallants lounging beneath the arcades.

Presently this costume will be worn by the heroines of the Fronde, the duchesses leagued against Mazarin, and afterwards, with certain alterations, it will become full dress costume at the splendid fêtes of the Court of Louis XIV.

Marion.

VII.

UNDER THE SUN-KING.

Under the Sun-King—From La Vallière to Maintenon—Gowns called 'transparent'—The triumph of Lace—The Romance of Fashion—Steinkirks—The Fontanges head-dress—The reign of Madame de Maintenon, or thirty-five years of moroseness.

I<small>T</small> is the reign of the Great King; the sovereignty of sumptuous ornament and majestic solemnity in architecture; it is also the reign of equally solemn and majestic wigs, and of fashions, amazingly luxurious indeed, but more superb than elegant.

"The great century!" Grandeur is pushed to pomposity, and splendour to ostentation; the same heavy magnificence prevails in the style of the hôtels or palaces wherein dwell bewigged nobles, and in their prim and pompous furniture, as in the dress of men and women, and the refined devices of fashion.

The great reign had a troubled prologue in the Fronde, which enabled the fine ladies to play at flirtatious politics, and to treat themselves to an idea of the emotions of their grandmothers in the days of the League. The strong hand which had held the reins of Government had dropped them, it was cold in death. Richelieu was gone; pranks were possible.

And what pranks did not the dukes, and the heroines of the Fronde proceed forthwith to play? This beginning of things, while as yet

A LA COUR DU ROI-SOLEIL.

the Great King was only the little king, has a prettily romantic air about it.

The Duchesses—Mme. de Chevreuse, Mme. de Montbazon, Mme. de Bouillon, Mme. de Longueville, and the Duchesse de Montpensier, Mademoiselle, "la Grande Mademoiselle," the granddaughter of Henri Quatre, who helped to beat the king's soldiers with cannon previously to being beaten herself with a cane by Lauzun, the handsome Lauzun, whom she took because she could not get Louis—all these fair and fascinating rebels, with their free manners, their fine figures, and their bright eyes, boldly assumed semi-military costumes, without going so far as the 'casaque' of the guards and the jacket[1] of the common soldiery.

During the years of trouble and disturbance, of civil war in Paris and armed cavalcades in the provinces, the ladies were present at the parades of the troops levied by the princes

[1] Hongreline (obsolete).

against the forces of the king, with Condé or against him. These charming amazons harangued the Parisian public (always ready for a rising) from the top of the steps of the Hôtel de Ville, addressing their fiery eloquence to a crowd bristling with old halberts and arquebuses that had belonged to the League, and they reviewed the forces of the Fronde (the city was by way of being besieged). In that Parisian militia, the cavalry 'des Portes Cochères,' and the 'Corinthian' regiment of M. le Coadjuteur, there still lingered traces of the picturesque bric-à-brac warrior of the time of the Duc de Guise. The warlike dames also valiantly turned the guns of the Bastille on the royal troops when things were going badly. What a pretty pretext for mannish modes!

Everything, fashion as well, was 'à la Fronde.' Fashion had good reason for a spite against Mazarin, who was renewing the prohibitive edicts, which were no sooner published than they were forgotten or defied, and which had to be constantly renewed. These absurd decrees denounced alternately gimp in favour of guipure, and guipure in favour of gimp.

Louis had grown up, and was reigning, but

A duchess of the Fronde.

the king was still young, and the Great Century was amusing itself; it liked glory, but it also liked pleasure. This was its early manner, in later days, the century and the king, both grown old, while still continuing to care for glory, bethought themselves of repenting of their pleasures.

The last Queen of Fashion, a queen austere and grim, who made the age do penance for all the frivolous inventions of her own fair youth, was that eminent refrigerator Mme. de Maintenon.

In the meantime, the fascinating Ninon de L'Enclos, la Vallière, Montespan, Fontanges, with many others, had reigned as queens or demi-queens for their little day.

The famous saying of Louis, "L'État c'est-moi!" might be put into the mouth of the Marquise de Montespan with respect to Fashion. With perfect truth she might have asserted, "La Mode c'est moi!" Nevertheless, feminine wits were constantly employed in inventing some ideal bit of finery, some pretty device for captivation, some new arrangement which Molière's exquisites should pronounce 'delicious.'

The men of the time wore 'canons,' 'rhin-graves' (those singular breeches in the form of beribboned petticoats), and 'petites oies'[1] of bunches of ribbon. Never were women more richly attired; both sexes expended money in dress with reckless lavishness.

There was no marked change in the general outlines of costume, but continual small alterations were made in details and ornament, constituting a succession of ephemeral fashions, all more or less costly and elegant, and known by a variety of picturesque names, such as gallants, ladders, 'fanfreluches' (little puffs of silks), transparents, furbelows, hurlyburlies, what-nots,[2] steinkirks, Fontanges, &c., &c.

Let us look at the portraits of the fair ladies of the Great Century, in its early years, the

---

[1] Littré explains this curious phrase as follows:

"*Petite-oie*, les bas, le chapeau, et les autres ajustements pour rendre un habillement complet ; ainsi dit par comparaison avec l'abatis d'une volaille." He quotes a sentence from *Les Précieuses Ridicules* of Molière : "Que vous semble-t-il de ma petite-oie ? La trouvez-vous congruente à l'habit ?"

[2] Prétintailles.

time of the 'ruelles' and the 'précieuses' of the Hôtel de Rambouillet, and also at those of the stars of the Sun-King's fêtes at the Tuileries or Versailles. At first the hair was worn in frizzed curls upon the forehead, and very large curls at either side of the face, or in long braids, tied by bows of ribbon styled 'gallants' and known as 'Cadenettes,' because the mode had been invented by M. de Cadenet, a brother of the Constable de Luynes, in the time of Louis XIII. The gowns were low-necked, liberally displaying the shoulders, necklaces of large pearls were worn, also the last of the lace bands ('rabats'), which became fine by degrees and beautifully less until they entirely disappeared; the pointed bodices were covered with embroidery, and the short sleeves ended in lawn ruffles or lace cuffs.

The outer skirt, which was raised like the sides of a window-curtain, and fastened by clasps set with brilliants, or by knots of ribbon, displayed the sumptuous under-dress.

Louis XIV. gave fashion its head by letting

the sumptuary edicts of Mazarin fall into desuetude. Prohibited lace reappeared, stuffs of forbidden richness were freely worn. The

Beginning of the great reign.

interdict remained upon cloth of gold and silver only, these the King reserved to himself and his Court. Louis made presents of pieces of those precious stuffs to highly-favoured personages, just as he granted jerkins 'by patent' to his favourite courtiers.

Madame de Montespan reigned after la Vallière. The dress she wore at one court festival in particular is described as—"A gown of gold on gold, broidered in gold, bordered with gold and over that gold frieze stitched with a gold mixed with a certain gold which makes the most divine stuff that has ever been imagined." This panegyric is from the pen of Madame de Sévigné.

'Transparent' gowns were much worn; they were of thin material, either muslin or lawn, with bunches of many-coloured flowers painted or printed on it, placed over an under-dress of bright-tinted moiré satin. In some instances the under-dress was composed of brocade, with large flowers on a gold or blue ground, with an upper gown of tissue as light as lace.

Lace was used in a variety of ways in every part of feminine attire, from the bodice to the shoes, mixing with the ribbon streamers which

SOUS LE GRAND ROI. — FIN DU XVIIe SIÈCLE.

tied the hair, forming the 'ladders' of large bows on bodices, bedecking petticoats, and floating about in all directions.

Lace manufactories sprang up everywhere,

Under the great king.

the 'points' (or stitches) of Alençon le Puy, Dieppe, Sedan, &c., were invented, lace-makers produced their wares at all sorts of prices, to suit the purses of duchesses and shopkeepers, from rich guipure costing hundreds of pistoles,

K

to be worn at Court by the Favourite, to the 'neigeuses' and 'gueuses' in which the lesser bourgeoises and even the market-women would appear on high days and holidays.

In 1680 a revolution in head-dresses took place. One day, at a royal hunting-party, the hat of the Duchesse de Fontanges (who had replaced Montespan in the favour of the Monarch), was blown off, and she employed her ribbon garter to confine her disordered locks, tying it in front with a smart rosette. Every thing a favourite does is of course charming and delightful. The fine gentlemen went into ecstasies over the 'inspiration,' the fine ladies were equally enchanted, and the next day everybody's hair was un-dressed à la Fontanges.

The Fontanges style became 'the rage,' and reigned for several years, but with alterations and additions. Ultimately it became an edifice of lace, ribbons, and hair, with the characteristic peak of lace mounted on brass wire, which Saint-Simon tells us was two feet high. Each article composing the structure had its distinctive name.

This fashion, which had so trifling an origin, lasted a long time, but at length it ceased to be pleasing to the King, who no doubt cared only for the severe style of Scarron's widow.

The Princess Palatine, Princess Charlotte of Bavaria, daughter of the Elector Palatine, came to France in 1671 to be married to Monsieur the King's brother—whose first wife was the daughter of Charles I. of England and Henrietta Maria—and set a fashion, by wearing a short cape to cover her shoulders, which were too much bared by the very low-cut bodices then worn. These little capes were speedily adopted by all the ladies, and were called 'palatines.'[1]

The romance of fashion, still gallant and heroic, now gives us Steinkirks, for it was the age of dandified chivalry, and bravery 'à la

---

[1] The mode was imported into England, where the capes were called 'pelerines,' the first of them having been made in fur.

mousquetaire.' "The position will be difficult to carry," said a colonel to his troops, just before a charge. "So much the better, gentlemen, we shall have all the more pleasure in telling our mistresses of the affair."

At the battle of Steinkirk, in which William of Orange was beaten by the Maréchal de Luxembourg, the Prince de Conti and the Duc de Vendôme, with Philip of Orleans, who was then only fifteen, charged with the cavalry; their dress was in disorder, their lace cravats being untied and flying in the wind. In the joy of victory the fashion of 'negligent' lace cravats was adopted, and all the women wore Steinkirks.

The wealthy country dames, and the ladies of the lesser nobility, imitated the modes and shapes of the Court costumes, and the bourgeoises followed suit at a humbler distance. Furetière in his bourgeois novel, and Sébastien Leclère in his etchings, show us "the imitative crew" with their coquettish ways, disdaining the homely hood of their mothers, wearing big 'bands' and pearl necklaces, bedizened bodices, and almost as great a quantity of lace and ribbons as the Court ladies

Early Fontanges head-dress.

displayed at Versailles. The rash Furetière even lets out that they were in the habit of borrowing diamonds for great occasions, and going to church with a borrowed lackey to carry the tail of their gowns.

Let us take Molière's serving-maid as a type of the woman of the people; she is a good girl. Sébastien Leclère has drawn her also with her plain coif, her raised skirt and her camisole with large basques, which is the 'hongreline,' or jacket of the soldiery of Louis Treize, afterwards adopted by ladies.

The shopkeepers and market-women whom he also drew wore wide bands and lace, with an air of dignity and majesty which proves that they too were of the 'great century.'

The brilliant and festive period of the reign of the Great King was in reality the shortest, the pivot turned in 1680, when Mme. de Maintenon, whom the King married privately five years later, began to acquire influence over him.

No more shall we go to the woods, all the roses are gathered, almost all the laurels also.

The reign of Mme. de Maintenon covered the respectable period of thirty-five years. Thus the Sun-King, whom we always picture to our fancy with the pomp and splendour of his youth around him, in all the lustre of his glory and gallantry, amid his be-ribboned courtiers, presiding over fêtes, balls, and carrousels, shining and shone upon by whole constellations of brilliant beauties—this great king became prematurely an old, morose, and bored monarch. It is true that he retained his taste for pomp, but with an affectation of formal solemnity, with, so to speak, a sumptuous severity.

The great century was a wearisome one, a time of gilded boredom in full dress and solemn wigs. The King, repenting him of the follies of his youth, and having turned to devotion and austerity, expected everybody else to do as he did.

Fashion changed at once. The dress of both men and women was simplified; ornaments that were considered too showy or too becoming, bright colours, and the flowered stuffs which had formerly charmed Court and City, disappeared, to give place to more discreet and sober attire.

This lasted until the time when Louis Quatorze himself, having had enough of his own moroseness and the prim coifs of Mme. de Maintenon, thought fit to request the fine gentlemen and the great ladies to revert to the display and splendour of former days, before devotion had become the fashion at his gloomy Court. It is needless to say that the royal invitation met with a joyful response, and that luxurious dress immediately reappeared.

The ladies of the close of the great century were dressed in splendid flowered stuffs gorgeously trimmed. The gowns, opening upon bodice fronts of fine lace, were of brocade or damask interwoven with gold, the skirts were raised and draped under a small apron of lace. The latter was not the most tasteful adjunct of their attire, it did not go well with outdoor dress.

The high points of the Fontanges head-dress were still to be seen, and the edifice had now become complicated and extravagant, with lace strings hanging at the back.

SOUS LA RÉGENCE.

Skirts were adorned with furbelows and 'prétintailles,' the former, invented by one Langlée, the son of a waiting-maid of the queen's, who had become the arbiter of taste

At the close of the great century.

and the oracle of fashion at Court, were rows of quilled flounces placed upon the straight skirt, but not on the loose-trained over-skirt, which was raised at the sides.

The 'prétintailles' of this period, were cut-out brocade flowers of all sizes and colours, applied to the material, a showy mode of decoration which made the wearers look as though they had made their gowns out of room-hangings or arm-chair covers.

Head-dress worn at home.

VIII.

THE EIGHTEENTH CENTURY.

The Regency—Follies and frivolities—Cythera at Paris—The Watteau fashions—'Flying' gowns—The birth of the panier—Criardes—'Considerations' and the Maîtres des Requêtes—Mme. de Pompadour—The Fan—The Promenade de Longchamps—Coaches and Chairs—Winter fashions.

FRANCE had experienced great trials and reverses after a long period of glory and magnificence, and was sorrowfully contemplating the slow and melancholy setting of the Sun-King. She had lived for many years in an atmosphere of oppressive ennui under the rule of the old monarch and the grim-visaged lady, his companion, and she realized with a sensible relief that Louis was in his vault at St. Denis, and Mme. de Maintenon in rigid retreat at St. Cyr. All the repressed youth, all the restrained frivolity, all the longing for pleasure of the whole nation revived, and the great madness of the Regency period broke out.

The frisky eighteenth century, kept in check under the rod of the grumbling and impotent old seventeenth, which seemed endless, was about to behave itself all of a sudden like an emancipated page, and to toss its cap very high indeed over all possible windmills.

Fashion, said by moralists to be the daughter of frivolity, invented a thousand new follies to do honour to its mother, and as though that were not enough, it re-adopted some of the old ones which had been so long forgotten that they were once more charming.

Fashion in the eighteenth century, from the Regency period onward, was characterized by breadth and amplitude, in fact by a return to the skirts of the time of Henri III., the farthingale with its consequences, width of sleeves and height of head-dresses, and these were soon to be exaggerated in virtue of a law of equilibrium and harmony.

Under Henri III., it was the ruff that grew up and forced the head into a portentous 'horn'; under Louis XV. and Louis XVI., it was the head-dress that became monumental.

The farthingale reappeared under the name of 'panier.' It came from the other side of the Channel. Two English ladies brought specimens to Paris, and exhibited them in the Garden of the Tuileries. The extravagant fullness of these ladies' skirts excited great surprise among the men and women who were taking their daily walk in the Gardens, a crowd gathered round the foreigners, and pressed on them so closely that they were in danger of being flattened, if not smothered. At length a gallant officer of the Mousquetaires du Roi interfered, and extricated the ladies and their paniers from a very unpleasant position.

At that time the fashions did not travel round the civilized world in six months, and disappear, without being entirely used up, in less than two seasons. They took time to come forth and be developed, and they lasted in their chief features, with the alterations, adjuncts, or improvements that were suggested every day, for several years.

The panier was destined to live throughout the century, and it took no less an event than the Revolution to kill it.

Some years elapsed before the farthingale completely reconquered Paris; its restoration was effected slowly, timidly, by modest attempts, then, one fine day, about 1730, it won, and its undisputed reign began. All the ladies, discarding half measures and demi-paniers, adopted the large panier, six feet in diameter, which took at least ten ells of stuff to cover it.

'Panier' was the self-evident name for this extraordinary article of costume, for the first petticoat extension was contrived by means of osier or cane hoops, bird-cages in fact; the whalebone arrangement came afterwards.

A Master of Requests whose name was

Regency hunting-costume.

Pannier having perished in a shipwreck on his voyage home from the Antilles, his sad fate was used by cruel fashion as a pretext for giving a nickname to the panier, just then in the dawn of its renown. Prior to this were the 'little Jansenist paniers,' coming down to the knee only; the 'creaker' (a bustle made of linen cloth, much gummed and folded), which creaked at the slightest movement; the 'call-bird,' the 'finger it,' the 'wench,' and the 'tumble.'[1] All these names were inventions of a time that was by no means prudish; there were also the more respectable small paniers called 'considerations.' For some time the large ones were called 'maîtres des requêtes.'

The large panier led naturally to a change in the make of gowns. Then arose those most graceful, dexterously-negligent fashions which we have called by the name of Watteau, in honour of the great painter of gala gallantry, on whose canvas so many of the fair ladies of his time survive "in hoops of wondrous size," painted and patched, fan or tall cane in hand, and always ready to embark for Cyprus with some red-heeled admirer.

[1] Criarde, boute-en-train, tâtez-y, gourgandine, culbute.

TOILETTE DE COUR LOUIS XV.

The real realm of Cythera was, however, Paris, whether governed by the Regent or by

Flying Gown.

Louis the Well-beloved. The century had fifty years before it, in which to gambol and amuse itself, fifty years for games and laughter, but the time would come when the powder and the patches were to be washed off by tears.

In this day of 'the unbraced cestus,' fashion invented loose gowns without either bodice or girdle, hanging straight from the shoulders over the wide-spread panier, or only fitted to the waist in front, and left quite loose with large folds at the back. This device gave the wearer an air of pretty carelessness and indolent grace, the distinguishing mark of the age.

The thick and heavy stuffs of the preceding period were unfit for these loose hanging gowns, and to drape the vastness of the paniers, so lighter fabrics were adopted, lawn, muslin, dimity, and other thin stuffs with bouquet patterns, or scattered flowers, or even little rural designs.

On fine days the promenades were crowded with ladies who looked as though they had come out in their morning costume, in gowns fashioned like dressing-gowns, their arms emerging from clouds of lace, and their faces from soft frills, as they waved their fans, and lazily clicked their high-heeled slippers.

It was the period of the Regency! There is a world of meaning in that word. The suppers and the orgies of the Palais-Royal were largely imitated elsewhere; there was many a Parabère in the gay and pleasure-loving city, which had just then been thrown into fresh excitement by the fever of speculation. Day after day the believers in John Law were either enriched or ruined; some making fabulous fortunes that enabled them to procure every kind and every degree of enjoyment, others being beggared, so that they had to drown their sorrows in dissipation at any cost.

The satirists of the pen had plenty of material in the loose gowns, the paniers, the head-dresses, the gew-gaws, all the daily inventions of fashion. Plays and songs, the Italian theatre, and the booth in the fair, caricatures and pamphlets, ridiculed the preposterous paniers, while the triumphant paniers mocked the mockers, and swelled themselves out more and more vaingloriously.

Everybody laughed or lamented. Here were several ladies to be accommodated in a coach which could only hold one with her balloon-skirt? Everything was too small; the streets were too narrow; salon-doors had to be widened to allow the overgrown ladies to pass in, just as it became necessary afterwards to make the doors higher at the top, so that the gigantic head-dresses of later days might enter without a hitch.

The arm-chairs were not big enough; how was a lady to sit down with those tremendous hoops, which either refused to be squeezed into the seat, or started up in the most embarrassing way?

Nevertheless, paniers went on growing larger until the early days of Marie Antoinette, and the skirts worn over them were laden more and more heavily with big and little flounces, lattice work, pleated frills, scallops, or ribbons arranged in a thousand different ways. These fashions were in some cases as pretty as

Large Panier.

they were complicated, but in others they were merely absurd.

Under the gown, which continued to be

worn loose and flowing for a long time, à la Watteau, the 'body' or corset strictly confined the bust, the satin bodice was pointed and the waist very long; as it was low-necked, a 'breast-front' of lace and ribbons protected the chest from cold.

Mantles were adapted to the season or the temperature; that is to say, they were either pretty little mantillas[1] which just covered the shoulders, with a light frilled silk or satin hood, or cloaks covering the entire figure down to the heels; the hood was held out by a hoop of brass wire around the head.

From 1725 to 1770 or 75, the fashion in gowns retained the same lines, and almost the same general arrangements, the swelling skirts, the clouds of lace, and the bunches of ribbon. The best period of the mode of the eighteenth century, that in which the Louis Quinze costume was at its highest point of elegance, was between 1750 and 1770, the middle period between the exaggeration of

[1] Coquéluchons (obsolete).

the Regency time and that of Louis XVI., which was no less unreasonable.

During those years her beautiful, astute, artistic, and encroaching majesty, Madame de Pompadour, reigned. If we would summon up a vision of that radiant period and realize its charm, we have but to quote the names

A little milliner.

of Boucher, Baudoin, La Tour, Lancret, Pater, Elsen, Gravelot, Saint-Aubin, and the whole galaxy of fops and exquisites, scented and silly indeed, but also delightfully polished and graceful.

There was corruption under the perfume of roses, it is true, and it will not do to scratch that vernis-Martin society too deeply; there was so much 'laisser-aller' and 'laisser-faire' everywhere, and it was so difficult to be scandalized by anything whatsoever.

After Pompadour, Louis XV. fell very low, even down to Dubarry; he had his seraglio at the 'Parc au Cerfs,' like the Grand Turk, his daughters, Loque, Chiffe, and Graille, drank brandy, and smoke pipes borrowed from the guard-room. Nobles and financiers had their "Follies," where they received great ladies or opera-girls, and marchionesses sat at table with Gardes-Françaises at Ramponneau's.

How skilfully this eighteenth century arranged its scenery and decorations, how carefully it laid out a pleasant and charming life for itself, never thinking or caring about that which awaited it in the fifth act of its fairy play! Its most exquisite personification is in Latour's great pastel, the portrait of Mme. de Pompadour, in a so-called 'négligé d'intérieur,' which is a poem in satin, ribbons, and lace.

PARISIENNE SOUS LOUIS XV.

THE EIGHTEENTH CENTURY. 153

Woman reigns and rules, the sceptre of her sovereignty is the fan. For a long time

Walking-dress.

the fan had been in use; in the middle ages it was called 'Esmouchoir'; there had been square fans, feather-fans attached by a jewelled chain to the girdles of noble ladies in the sixteenth century, and the folded fan, brought from Italy by Catherine de Médicis, and adopted by Henri III.

From the time of Louis XIV., the fan had been indispensable to the toilet of women, but its great period, in which the finest specimens were produced, was the eighteenth century.

The Louis Quinze fans, with their ivory and mother-of-pearl mounts, marvellously cut and worked, and their exquisite paintings by Watteau, Lancret, and others, were the sceptres of a powdered, effeminate, and affected society; wielded by the hands of favourites, the fan swayed the monarch, his ministers and generals, the arts, letters, politics, and the world.

The engraving by Gabriel de Saint-Aubin, entitled 'Le Bal Paré,' shows us the fine ladies of that time in full dress; still the Watteau folds, the loose gowns open over the bodice and under-skirt, caught in at the waist by ribbons, and raised high at the sides on the swell of the panier, still the profusion of fluttering trimmings, borders of fur or folded bands, and flounces of satin or lace.

After G. de Saint-Aubin.

Head-dresses began to mount up again, but were still elegant and becoming, the powdered hair was raised over the well-displayed forehead, and arranged in bows and rolls mingled with loops of ribbon, feathers, and pearls.

Let us glance at these same ladies at the Promenade de Longchamps, in superb painted and gilded coaches, for that was the carriage-building time of fairy tale, and compared with its productions, the most sumptuous vehicles of our prosaic epoch, however well "turned out," varnished, and blazoned, would look like hearses.

In these imposing carriages, driven by stately coachmen, bewigged, belaced, and befrogged, with tall footmen in showy liveries hanging on behind, what a display there was of luxurious dress, lace, feathers, ribbons, diamonds and pearls!

Grooms rode at the carriage doors, running-footmen pushed through the crowd of equipages and equestrians of both sexes. In the crowd assembled on both sides of the road to admire the fashionable beauties, and fashion itself, amid the chatter of casual meetings, and conversations with young nobles, dandies, and

After the younger Moreau.

roués, the 'marquise,' and the 'présidente,' the lady of quality and the lady of 'finance,' the opera-girl, the dancer, the actress of the hour, who was turning the empty heads of the play-going gallants who vied with each other for her favour, and the courtesan who might next week be proclaimed 'Queen by the left hand,' elbowed each other promiscuously.

When winter came, these fine ladies would forsake their coaches, and that other delightful creation of a charming age, the Sedan chair (*chaise à porteurs*), painted in vernis-Martin with scenes of gallantry or pastoral life in the styles of Boucher and Watteau; they would lay aside laces and ribbons, wrap themselves up in furs, and be off, their little pink noses just peeping out of sable or blue fox, and their hands hidden in muffs as big as drums, to drive on the snow in splendid sleighs of extraordinary shapes, brilliantly painted, ornamented with carved and gilded figures, and elegant and fanciful beyond description.

Large Louis Seize hat.

IX.

EIGHTEENTH CENTURY—LOUIS XVI.

Enormous head-dresses—The pouf 'au sentiment'—Parks, kitchen-gardens, and landscapes with figures, worn on the head—The 'Belle-Poule' head-dress—Patches—Country fashions—'Negligent' gowns—Fashionable colours—Riding-habits—English fashions—The bourgeoises.

THE century was growing old; the age of exquisite coquetry, of powdered and perfumed elegance, was becoming stricken in years, and waxing weary of its butterfly air and its tinsel decoration.

Taste had grown tired and was indolent, novelty was no longer sought for, fashion remained stationary for a long time, or moved in a circle only.

The Louis Quinze style was now out of date, like that of Louis Quatorze; 'rococo' was pronounced to be 'perruque' and 'vieux jeu'; but let us wait a bit, fashion is about to spread its wings suddenly and to risk everything, even a tumble into the preposterous; but surely it may allow itself to do this three or four times in a century, after all ?

The little seed of folly which always lurks in the frivolous and topsy-turvy brain of the goddess of fashion, was about to sprout. While still retaining the beautiful and becoming Pompadour and Watteau forms for a while, the mode was preparing to work its wild will upon head-dresses, to take women's heads for the parade-ground of its maddest whims, to

GRANDS PANIERS LOUIS XVI.

load them with the most absurd inventions under the pretext of beautifying them, to transform them into landscapes, or indeed into sea-pieces, then to befeather the latter, raise them up to a fabulous height, and erect edifices upon them, with little cardboard figures of men and women to complete the absurdity.

Then would Paris swarm with hair-dressers of genius, the Legros and the Léonards, the Raphaels and the Rubenses, or rather the Soufflots of the barber's art, and these personages would set up academies for teaching the principles of their capillary architecture; striving who should attain the utmost perfection of the ridiculous in the adornment of aristocratic heads, and all succeeding pretty equally in reaching it.

The wigmakers had already had their day of glory and renown in the great century, that of the majestic peruke; having now become academicians of hair-dressing, they were about to secure a fresh triumph, at the expense of feminine grace.

M

Let us observe the lady of the period at her toilette, preparing to make her calls, or to go to the Tuileries at the fashionable hour. This laboratory business, for so it must be reckoned, is the important affair of the day, it means the adjustment of mere beauty to the prevalent taste. The toilette hour, after the 'petit lever,' has been delineated by Lancret, Baudoin, and the other gallant or elegant painters of the age, with all the skill that they possessed, and the caricaturists have not refrained from depicting it either.

Madame, seated before her mirror—its frame is carved and gilded—in the dressing-closet with its white wood panels, moulded and carved in the style called 'rock-work,' has been dressed by her women; at her 'petit lever' she has given audience to her admirers and her milliners, to the marquis and the banker, to the poet who extols her charms in the *Almanach des Muses*, to the flippant 'chevalier,' and the gallant Court Abbé.

"What does the Abbé say?" The Abbé is

a person of taste, and his opinion upon everything connected with the freaks of fashion is valuable.

But all these frivolous people have been dismissed, it is the hair-dresser's hour, the serious, the only really important moment of the day.

The artist needs to be alone, lest his inspiration should be put to flight, and besides, the task is long, difficult, and requires much care and preparation to render it successful. He can tolerate one or two waiting-women who understand him at half a word, and hand him everything he requires while he is in the fine frenzy of composition, but no other spectator.

According to the rank of the lady, this hair-dresser will be the great artist, who comes in his coach, passing swiftly from hôtel to hôtel in the noble Faubourg, and expected at the Tuileries, or by some princess, or else he will be one of the great artist's pupils, operating in a dress-coat, with lace ruffles and a sword by his side.

The inspiration comes, and under the fingers, the comb, and the curling-tongs of the artist an extraordinary structure of natural curls, skilfully mingled with enormous quantities of borrowed hair, is built up in stages, on which are piled bows, 'frizzes,' 'gates,' 'chestnuts,' 'crutches,' &c., for these extraordinary names were given to the inventions of the hair-dressers.

For twenty years this medley of strange constructions under pretence of hair-dressing went on. Folly had taken up its abode on the heads of women. Among the most preposterous inventions, I may enumerate the 'Quesaco,' the 'Monte-au-ciel' (the name indicates its proportions), the 'Comète,' the 'Hérisson à quatre boucles' (or 'Hedgehog with four curls,' invented by Marie Antoinette, who outdid the exaggeration of fashion), the 'Parterre galant.' Then we have the Cradle of Love and the Novice of Venus, as names for hats of outrageous size and shape.

Poufs were bewildering things; the 'pouf au sentiment' was an absurd arrangement of

EIGHTEENTH CENTURY—LOUIS XVI. 165

A courtesan, after Wille.

flowers and shrubs, with birds in the branches, growing on a high hill of hair; butterflies and Cupids flew about this garden. There were

Court dress.

also the 'pouf à la chancelière,' or foot-muff pouf, the 'pouf à droite,' and the 'pouf à gauche.'

The 'pouf au sentiment' allowed great

latitude to invention, and the display of feeling and taste. The Duchesse de Chartres, mother of King Louis-Philippe, wore on her pouf a miniature museum of little images, her eldest son in his nurse's arms, a little negro, a parrot nibbling a cherry, and designs executed in the hair of her nearest and dearest kinsfolk.

After the 'garden' hair-dressing, we find the 'Cascade of Saint-Cloud' style, consisting of a cataract of powdered ringlets falling from the top of the head, the 'kitchen-garden' style, with bunches of vegetables hooked in to the side-curls, the 'rural' style, with landscapes representing a hill-side, windmills which actually turned, a meadow crossed by a silver stream, with a shepherdess tending her sheep, mountains, a forest with a sportsman and his dog in pursuit of game, &c., &c.

Then came the 'Coliseum,' the 'Innocence,' the 'Peal of bells,' the 'Bobwig,' the 'Milkmaid,' the 'Bather,' the 'Kerchief,' the 'Neckerchief,' the 'Oriental,' the 'Circassian,' the 'Minerva's helmet,' the 'Crescent,' the

'Bandeau of Love,' and among hats, the 'Enigma,' the 'Desire to please,' the 'Turned-up Calash,' the 'Pilgrim Venus,'[1] the 'Treasurer of the age,' 'Frivolous Bather,' &c., while hair-curling was done in 'sustained sentiments,' or 'sentiments recalled.'

The full-dress head-gear, a great scaffolding bedecked with feathers and flowers in tufts and garlands, was so large and so heavy, and took up so much space, that ladies, who already found it difficult to get their paniers into their carriages, had to hold their heads down on one side, or even to kneel on the floor of the vehicle.[2]

Caricatures of the period represent ladies wearing these monstrous head-dresses in Sedan chairs, with the roof taken off to allow the top of the gigantic structure, powdered to an Alpine whiteness, to come through.

The most amazing of all these inventions was the 'Belle-Poule,' so called in honour of

[1] Pilgrim Venus apparently means Venus with her cockle-shell, an antique design.
[2] See note, Appendix, p. 263.

PARISIENNES 1789.

the victory of the frigate *La Belle Poule* over *The Arethusa*, an English ship, in 1778. Upon the great mass of hair arranged in rolling waves, was placed a frigate in full sail, with

Head-dress à la Belle Poule.

all its masts, yards, guns, and little sailors. After having composed such a master-piece, Léonard or Dagé might go hang themselves, they could never beat that.

It was in '89 that the ridiculous head-gear of women reached its utmost absurdity. The highest of them all set the example. Alas! she had to expiate her fault and her folly! The head had sinned, the head paid the penalty, and if the loftiest of all fell, it was through the fault of the very person who had tempted her with his eccentric inventions during her prosperous years.

Léonard, the 'illustrious' hair-dresser to the Queen, was one of the party who went to Varennes. At that terrible moment, in the great shipwreck of the monarchy, the object was to secure—what? The services of the indispensable Léonard. That last weakness of hers turned out ill for the poor Queen, for, it is said, some erroneous information given (quite innocently) to a detachment of the troops commanded by the Marquis de Bouillé, by Léonard, who had preceded the royal fugitives, was the cause of the disaster of Varennes, where the expected aid was missing.

When the fashionable lady's hair had been

dressed, she hid her face in a large paper bag, while a thick coating of powder was applied to the structure—what a strange fashion it was that shed the snow of years on the heads of

Large Pouf.

young and old alike—and then, her cheeks being rouged to the right colour, forming a harsh contrast with the plastered white hair—'rouge,' said Madame de Sévigné, " is all the law and the prophets"—she needed only to put on the patches which were intended to bring out certain points of physiognomy, and give piquancy to expression, in order to be quite irresistible.

These patches, which women were careful to place in the most becoming manner, each according to her special style of beauty, bore the following amusing names—

The 'majestic' was placed on the forehead, the 'funny' at a corner of the mouth, on the lips of a brunette the patch was 'the roguish,' on the nose it was 'the saucy,' in the middle of the cheek 'the gallant,' near the eye, as it rendered the glance either languid or passionate, according to the fair one's intention, it was 'the murderous,' while the fanciful patches, crescents, stars, comets, hearts, etc., were past counting.

But we are coming to the last days of a world about to go to pieces, of a society about to disappear in a sudden catastrophe.

From 1785 the old régime was in a tottering

state; the revolution was an accomplished fact—in dress.

It was a complete revolution, and it came almost without transition, the gay and gallant costume of the eighteenth century was aban-

Head-dress worn at home.

doned for a series of new inventions which imparted totally different lines to the form.

"Adieu paniers, vendanges sont faites." The well-known phrase, applicable at some time to all earthly things, was never more appropriate. The enormous paniers ceased to exist, at first they had been replaced by elbow-paniers (à coude), consisting of a roll attached to two short pieces of padding, worn on either side, and serving as a support for the elbows, and a third roll at the back—in short a bustle. But this compromise was soon rejected, and women in almost flat skirts approached little by little to the 'sheath' gown, and the too simple apparel of the Revolution.

Marie Antoinette, playing at farming at Trianon, brought a touch of peasant costume into fashion, of course it was peasant costume of the comic opera kind, shepherdess dress in the sense of Florian or 'Le Devin du Village.' Straw hats, aprons, short jackets, and bed-gowns made their appearance.

Léonard reigned over heads, and ruled them after his fancy; in other things Mlle. Rose Bertin, the great purveyor of fashion to the Queen (she was called her "Minister of Modes"), was the supreme arbiter of taste at the Court of Marie Antoinette.

Rose Bertin issued orders and made decrees,

she invented and composed; the ladies declared everything that came out of her hands to be a marvel, and their husbands complained of

A large hat.

the magnitude of her charges—as husbands always do.

About 1780 there came a turn of the tide of fashion, and new shapes were demanded.

Polish and Circassian gowns, which had nothing either Polish or Circassian about them, were invented; these gowns were short at first, and looped up on paniers, afterwards they were long and flowing.

The tendency towards 'negligent' fashion increased, 'Lévite' gowns[1] came in, and gave rise to a disturbance in the Garden of the Luxembourg. A certain countess appeared there in a 'Monkey-tailed levite,' that is to say a gown with a curiously cut and twisted train; she was followed by a mocking crowd, and the guard had to be called to her rescue.

After the 'Lévites,' came 'negligent,' and 'half-negligent,' 'chemise,' 'bather's,' and 'undress' gowns.

The fashionable colours for these oddly-named garments were—

'Canary's tail,' 'agitated nymph's thigh,' 'carmelite,' 'dauphin,' 'newly-arrived people,'

---

[1] A 'Lévite' was a long straight frock-coat, like that worn by priests; the 'Robe-lévite' imitated it, with the train added. The word is obsolete.

PROMENADE PARISIENNE 1790.

'lively shepherdess,' 'green apple,' 'stifled sigh.'

Lévite Robe.

A flea had somehow come to Court, the guard at the gates of the Louvre notwithstanding—

immediately there was a 'flea' (*puce*) series;
'flea-belly,' 'flea-back,' 'flea-thigh,' 'old flea,'
'young flea,' etc.[1]

The flea-colours suddenly gave place to
another tint which was also of courtly origin,
but bore the more seemly name, 'hair of the
Queen,'[2] conferred upon it by the Comte
d'Artois. On the instant every stuff had to
be 'hair of the Queen' colour.

The dress in which women rode on horseback,
called 'Amazone,' was not, in the eighteenth
century, the gloomy black garment inflicted
upon the world by modern taste, and aggravated
by the hideous tall hat.

Moreau the younger, whose series of engravings in *Le Monument de Costume* shows us
the whole of the society of his time, in the midst
of its fêtes, its ceremonies, and its pleasures, in
the salon, in the boudoir, in country-houses, at
the Court, at the opera, in the Bois de Boulogne,

[1] The King, Louis XVI., is said to have bestowed this name on the new colour.
[2] Cheveu de la Reine.

everywhere, has drawn the fine ladies of 1780 in riding-dress, with long skirts and belts, English over-coats and little waistcoats, and large hats perched atop of the powdered

An 'Amazon,' after the younger Moreau.

Cadogan[1] plait which is familiar to us in these latter days.

The riding-habits of the eighteenth century

[1] See note, Appendix, p. 264.

were very becoming, and admitted of great variety; certainly the crowd in the Avenue of the Champs-Elysées did not then present the gloomy aspect which it wears at present even on the finest spring days.

Was it in reprisal for the war in America, that the monarchy was invaded by British fashions during the last years of its existence? The shapes were new, and, both in general outlines and in detail, the preceding fashions were disregarded. Dress assumed unceremonious airs and an English 'cachet,' which implied a new régime. The 'only wear' included vests, jackets with waistcoats, 'frocks' with big buttons or laced, and 'driving coats' with large lapels and triple collars, tight to the figure and very long at the back. The large and showy buttons of the vests were in metal of every kind and shape, and sometimes adorned with little pictures; there are curious samples of these in various collections.

Women as well as men of fashion wore two watches with two long chains hanging from the

EIGHTEENTH CENTURY—LOUIS XVI.

waistcoat; they also wore cravats, Cadogans, and

English fashions.

'clubs' like men, and carried long canes, while men took kindly to the women's big muffs.

And the fichu! All women wore, with every

kind of dress, large fichus, which swelled out the chest to an unnatural extent above the long and horribly-squeezed waist.

These costumes hoisted all the colours of the rainbow, the lightest, the brightest, the strangest; there were satins, silks, and cloths of lemon colour, pink, apple green, canary, shot Indian silks, muslins, either plain or striped, of every possible tint. Stripes had an immense success in 1787. During the summer of that year, men, women, and children, all wore striped costumes.

Head-dressing also joined the revolutionary movement. The birth of the modern bonnet was at hand, head-costume, as understood by the nineteenth century, was about to develope itself. Women were still powdered, and still wore an immense quantity of hair in enormous wigs which bulged out around their faces, in the style of the masculine peruke, with big curls hanging at either side of the neck and down the back, or, like men, a thick club or Cadogan behind the head. Hats were of extraordinary

EIGHTEENTH CENTURY—LOUIS XVI.

shapes and dimensions, with immense brims, and enormous crowns laden with an extravagant quantity of trimming. A frigate in full sail

The bonnet-hat.

was no longer worn on the head, but a boat, keel upward, put on sideways, and big enough to serve as an umbrella on occasion, was the height of fashion.

The bonnet-hat, and the demi-bonnet, a little smaller, but of the same height, were trimmed with bows of ribbon, ruches, and tufts of cock's feathers. The turban-hat, a tall Janissary's cap, was striped, plumed, and trimmed with a gauze scarf; the hat, called for the sake of the satirical pun, 'à la Caisse d'escompte,' because it was 'sans fonds,' was made of open straw, the hat which came into fashion after the affair of the Necklace, and was called 'Cardinal sur la paille' (à propos of Cardinal de Rohan), made of straw edged with ribbon of Cardinal red. The big hat 'à la Tarare,' the 'Basile,' invented after the success of Beaumarchais, and many other fashions à la Figaro, the 'Widow of Malabar,' the Montgolfier cap, the 'Fixed Globe,' the 'Balloon'— these latter in honour of the first aerostatic experiments which made the sensation of the moment—preceded the cap 'of the Three Orders,' with which the long series of revolutionary fashions began, on the Assembly of the States-General.

In this eighteenth century, which was nearing

so dismal a close, there were, besides the belles of the Court and the capital, the more or less great ladies — for the demi-monde already

Turban hat.

existed—the famous dancers, and the celebrated courtesans, besides the queens of fashion who went to Longchamps attended by a turbaned footman to carry their parasols, and preceded by a running footman in tights and a plumed cap, with a long gold-tipped cane in his hand, besides the bedizened dames who followed every freak of the capricious mode, many charming women of the bourgeoisie,—we may trace them in old portraits, and in the minor Memoirs—who did not cover themselves with feathers and lace, but dressed with taste and discretion, following fashion at a wise distance, and discreetly preserving the old traditions and the old attire.

These were the fair women who wore little coifs, so different from the pyramids of hair and trumpery built up by Léonard, exquisitely becoming and pretty under a hood stiffened with wire; these were the women who wore modestly-cut gowns and small hoops, and who eschewed furbelowed paniers twenty feet in circumference.

These were the women who retained the purity of the good old ways and morals, in a licentious age, who led calm and dutiful lives, treading the narrow paths of household occupations and simple pleasures, going to their religious duties on Sundays and feast-days, and to such homely entertainments and country-

1789.

parties as came in due course in their quiet existence.

Theirs, too, was a world nearing its end, in the fusion and confusion of classes in the great revolutionary caldron, first in the political, and afterwards in the industrial and scientific revolution, that vast upturning and overthrow which was to result for us all in the feverish and breathless life of our own epoch.

Meanwhile, the women on whom we turn a passing glance, the worthy, simple women of the lesser bourgeoisie, never dreamed of the troublous time that was so near, saw nothing of that terrible blood-cloud, which was gathering upon the horizon, but would sing with light hearts to their harpsichords in their little white salons some pretty little sentimental air, very different from our complicated musical logarithms.

> Plaisir d'amour ne dure qu'un moment,
> Chagrin d'amour dure toute la vie.

Charlotte Corday Cap.

X.

THE REVOLUTION AND THE EMPIRE.

Fashions called 'à la Bastille' — Fashions of the Revolution — Notre-Dame de Thermidor—'Incroyables' and 'Merveilleuses'—Antiquity in Paris—'Athenian' and 'Roman' women—A pound of clothes—Transparent tunics—Tights, bracelets, and buskins—The reticule or ridicule—'The Victims' Ball—Blonde wigs and dog's ears—'À la Titus'—'Robes-fourreau'—Little caps and Hats—Shakos—Turbans.

THE hurricane which was destined to sweep as a cyclone over our ancient Europe for twenty-five years, already blew upon Paris, whence it took its origin, shaking and demolishing all before it. A monarchy that had lasted for centuries was about to fall amidst the débris of the old order, like a Bastille or a house of cards.

During this time, while the slaughterers were carrying heads about on pikes, while the new masters of France at the Assembly or the Commune were deciding the fate of millions of men about to be set in battle array, while already, in that ominous dawn of a new age, the new queen, the Guillotine, had risen in her might and spread her blood-red arms over her people, imperturbable Fashion was busy with fresh contrivances, altering the cut of skirts, arranging bodices, twisting ribbons into previously-unknown knots, inventing idyllic toilettes of exquisite novelty, for must not a new nation have new costumes?

The change that set in during the last peaceful years of Louis Seize gathered speed and character. Fashion had struck into a new path, and little by little all the characteristics of the former time, the old régime, as it is called, disappeared.

In the famous print by Debucourt, *La Promenade publique*, which gives us a vivid vision of a crowd of fine folk in the early days of the Revolution, what remains of the costumes and modes of the century among that charming assemblage of belles and beaux, who seem wholly unconcerned with the great drama? Powder, a few shovel-hats on the heads of a few old men, who lag behind the time, and that is all.

The aspect of women was strangely altered. English fashions prevailed at first, that is to say waistcoats and riding-habits were worn, but afterwards gowns became more simple, both in make and material.

Times were hard, good-bye to rich tissues, to silks and satins, to the costly gear of former days. Cotton, Indian print, and lawn replaced silk, and dressmakers adhered to straight lines with little ornament and few accessories. Lawn bodices were made chemise-wise, leaving the arm bare from the elbow, skirts were plain, almost flat, and had long sashes. This extreme simplicity was relieved by the national colours, trophies, and revolutionary symbols, imprinted on the stuff, or a scanty frill was added to the edge of the skirt.

Large muslin fichus were still worn, and on great occasions the costume was completed by a bunch of tricolored flowers placed on the left side above the heart, and by patriotic trinkets, neck-lockets, waist-buckles, in steel or copper, cockades, earrings, buttons 'à la Bastille,' 'au Tiers-État,' 'à la Constitution,' &c. For a while everything was 'à la Bastille,' even the hats.

The large cone-shaped hats with wide brims, and over-laden with ribbons, after having tried to hold out for some time, disappeared; then came a spell of caps only—caps with great puffed and be-ribboned crowns, caps like the head-tires of the women of Caux in Normandy, especially the 'peasant' and 'milkmaid' caps and the graceful coif with wide lace borders,

MERVEILLEUSE EN TUNIQUE A LA GRECQUE.

which we now call the 'Charlotte Corday cap,' mounting a large tricolour cockade.

Hardly any white powder was used—so much black was about to be consumed—the hair was worn as it grew, with a little added, but white wigs were just 'coming in.'

Dog's ears.

Soon, however, the tempest broke out in earnest. The Terror had begun. Could there be any further question of luxury, frivolity and fashion? The ranks of fine ladies were thinned, they were in the Abbaye, in La Force, in a hundred prisons, or at Coblentz;—they were in hiding, or they were dead.

The extreme simplicity affected by everybody, either from motives of prudence, or because it was impossible to care about dress at such a time, did not always suffice to avert the appellation of 'suspect,' which was a sure passport to the scaffold. Talleyrand said that those who had not lived in the old society of former times did not know the sweetness of living. In '93, the problem was to live, no matter in what seclusion, like a mouse in a hole, if necessary. Under this gentle reign of Liberty, the law ordained that a placard should be placed on every house, setting forth the names of all the inhabitants, and even their ages; this was a hard enactment. Many harmless people who had known bright and happy days endeavoured to shut out the mutterings of the storm, the tumult of the streets, and the horrible clamour of clubs and newspapers, in obscure apartments in silent and sleepy streets. Nevertheless, a small group yet hoisted the standard of dress in the face of the Sans-culottes. These brave men and women still displayed elegant attire, at the Palais-Royal, on the boulevards, at the prome-

The Hussar hat.

nades, and at such of the theatres as remained open, braving the citizens in carmagnoles and red caps, and the knitting hags of the guillotine. But, at how great a risk was this done! Fashion did not dare to struggle any longer, the poor thing hid its head under its wing, and hoped for a better day.

The guillotine was always at work, interrupted only from time to time by some idyllic festival, the fête of the Supreme Being, of Agriculture, or of Old Age, with rows of young girls in white, goddesses of Liberty, choruses of old men and boys, charming pastorals, spectacles which sweetly stirred the hearts of the good Marat and the sensitive Robespierre. Sand was strewn over the blood for the day, on the morrow the red stream began to run again.

Ninth Thermidor! For love of Citizeness Thérèse Cabarrus, a star about to rise, Tallien had braved death, then hanging over every head. He had defeated Robespierre, and flung him in his turn into the impassive arms of the goddess Guillotine.

Mme. Tallien became Notre-Dame de Thermidor, she who saves by the sovereign power of beauty!

A deep sigh of relief was heaved by all France, and immediately the repressed and terrorized powers lifted up their heads; forth came dress and fashion, with luxury, with frivolity, and even folly, with gladness, and laughter. Yes, there was a frantic longing for laughter after so much blood and weeping.

The 'Incroyables,' and the 'Merveilleuses,' who had already appeared before the Terror, displayed themselves in crowds on the promenades and boulevards, and Fashion, whose head had no doubt been turned by the Robespierre régime, though still pale with fear, began at once to revel in countless follies.

While the fops belonging to the 'gilded youth' of Paris, and appropriately called 'Incroyables,' with their high-collared coats, their huge cravats and the twisted sticks that were so necessary for their defence against Jacobins and terrorist sectionaries, imitated English fashions, the 'Merveilleuses' were unanimous in the worship of antiquity. For some years there were no more Parisians, all the women were Greek and Roman.

Straight gowns without waists, mere sheaths bound around the bosom by a girdle, short in front to let the foot be seen, slightly trained at the back, such was the attire of the 'Merveilleuses.' Nothing but antiquity was known; everything had begun over again.

During the Terror, modesty had been forgotten; this Athenian costume was merely a second chemise, and might have passed, but for the jewellery that was worn with it, for a symbol of the poverty of that time of ruin, when the louis d'or was worth eight hundred livres in assignats. It was a tunic of transparent lawn, which clung to the wearer's body with each movement. In addition to this, the diaphanous tunics of the leaders of fashion were slit down the sides from the hips.

Notre-Dame de Thermidor, Thérèse Cabarrus, now Citizeness Tallien, the Queen of Fashion, appeared at Frascati, dressed, or, rather, undressed, in the classic style; her

Athenian gown showed her legs clad in flesh-coloured tights with golden circlets for garters,

A Merveilleuse.

antique buskins, and rings on each toe of her statue-like foot.

In the salons, in the summer-gardens, at the promenades, the only wear was this antique gown, open above and below, worn with 'Carthaginian' chemises, or even without any chemise at all, sandals and buskins fastened by narrow red bands, gold circlets set with precious stones, 'arrangements' of tunics and peplums, corset-belts a couple of inches wide close under the bosom and adorned with brilliants.

The fluttering gowns allowed the legs to be seen, or even, when not slit open at the side, were raised above the knee, and, fastened with a cameo brooch, boldly displaying the left leg. Very little sleeve was worn, a mere strap, or even no sleeves at all, the edges of the gown were drawn together by cameos on the shoulders, and the arms were laden with bracelets.

As it was impossible to put pockets into these flimsy tunics, the ladies adopted the use of the 'balantine,' or 'reticule" (which was immediately pronounced 'ridicule'), an old name for a little bag ornamented with spangles or embroidery, and shaped like a hussar's

MERVEILLEUSE DU DIRECTOIRE.

sabretache; in this the handkerchief and purse were carried. Jacob the Bibliophilist relates that on a certain evening, in a fashionable salon under the Directory, everybody being eloquent in admiration of a costume so truly antique that nothing except the mode of the Garden of Eden could be more so, the fortunate wearer laid a wager that it did not weigh two pounds. Proof was given, the lady retired into a boudoir, and her entire costume with the trinkets was found to weigh little over one pound.

This neo-Athenian dame might count herself very much dressed, for others found means to be still less encumbered with clothes, and actually ventured to exhibit themselves in a costume called 'The female Savage,' which consisted solely of a gauze chemise over pink fleshings with golden garters.

Women actually walked in the Champs-Elysées in 'sheaths' almost entirely transparent, or even with the bosom completely bared, and these women were not courtesans, but belonged to the official 'world' of the day, and were friends of Joséphine de Beauharnais.

This was thoughtlessness rather than immodesty, a passing fit of insanity, the delirium of pleasure after furious madness and the delirium of blood!

The 'Merveilleuses,' who had defied the guillotine, also defied disease. Nevertheless, many of these foolish half-naked women were seized with pleurisy and inflammation of the lungs on leaving crowded ball-rooms and salons, after dancing, with no more protection from the cold of the night than a thin fichu or a shawl no larger than a scarf. Having taken their costume fashions from Athens, these semi-draped fine ladies borrowed their head-dresses from Greek statues, and wore their crisply-curled hair in a net, the tresses and plaits having jewels inserted in them. But the 'rage' was for fair-haired wigs. Mme. Tallien had thirty, of every shade of light hair. These wigs, which were slightly powdered, had been abhorred and proscribed by the Jacobins; after Thermidor

came their triumph, the 'peruke blonde' was
thenceforth a symbol of the counter-revolution.

For a while hair was dressed 'à la Victime,'
or 'à la Sacrifiée;' being combed up at the
back and brought forward on the forehead
in wild locks. This guillotine style of head-
dress, with a blood-red ribbon round the
neck, and a shawl of the same colour on the
shoulders, was indispensable for all those who
appeared at the famous and ghastly 'Bal des
Victimes,' to which neither man nor woman was
admitted who could not prove that either of
his or her parents, or some near relation, had
died upon the scaffold in the Terror.[1]

"Paole d'honneu victimée, ces dames sont
déliantes!" said the 'Incroyables,' in the
fashionable slang, and with the lisp à la mode,
to each new invention, more 'delicious' and more
'antique' than the preceding, of Mme. Nancy
and Mme. Raimbout, a pair of learned and
artistic dressmakers, who employed sculptors
to assist them in devising methods of draping

[1] See note, Appendix, p. 264.

more and more Greek, and folds increasingly Roman.

Roman fashions, which were somewhat less light and loose, were adopted by ladies who shrank from the too literal transparency of the Flora and the Diana tunics.

Roman gowns were worn by the ladies of the official world, who considered themselves bound to exercise a certain discretion, but the two worlds effected a fusion. Light and frivolous 'Athenians,' remains of the old and parvenus of the new society, army contractors or suddenly enriched speculators, 'muscadins' and 'muscadines,' victims and persecutors, gilded youth, the army, politics, and finance, all these formed the most marvellous of mixtures after the great shock, and rejoiced in the happiness of living after the great slaughter, notwithstanding the troubles of the present, and the uncertainty of the future.

A sudden decree of fashion put an end to the fair wigs, and imposed the 'Titus' on all women with any pretensions to a place in its ranks. The Directory belles threw away their perukes, and also sacrificed their own locks. No more hair, or at any rate as little as possible!

"The Titus mode," says La Mésangère in *Le bon Genre*, the official organ of Fashion, "consists in having the hair cut close to the

Titus Coiffure.

roots, so as to restore its natural stiffness to the tube, and make it grow in a perpendicular direction." 'Merveilleuses' and 'Muscadins' each and all adopted the 'Titus,' and were closely shorn, a few long dishevelled locks being allowed to hang over the brow.

There was yet another type of 'Merveilleuses' under the Directory. This was the 'Merveilleuse à la Carle Vernet,' still lightly clothed, still squeezed into a thin clinging skirt of 'Fie! Fie! pale startled' colour,[1] but wearing above her bodice (which was so small as to be almost invisible), and above her naked bosom, a formidable cravat, in whose folds her neck was enveloped several times, precisely like the muscadin's, while from beneath her huge plumed hat long locks of hair hung like dog's ears about her face.

Such was the attire and the head-dress of beaux and belles at the dawn of our century. During the Consulate and the first years of the Empire, the 'Merveilleuses' were a little, but not much, more clothed than under the Directory. The same gowns, frequently transparent, continued to be worn, necks continued to be bared to excess in all seasons. The women of that time went out walking in the day, as the women of our time go to balls,

[1] Fifi pâle effarouché.

with their bosoms and arms exposed. Their defence against cold consisted of scarfs and shawls — the forerunners of those famous

Under the Consulate.

'Cachemires,' which played so great a part in the first half of the century.

Special garments were invented, such as the little hussar vest, in 1808, which was put on over the low-necked bodice, and encircled the shoulders with its fur border, also the far less becoming spencer.

The celebrated portrait of Joséphine de Beauharnais by David, and that of Mme. Récamier by Gérard, shew us two beautiful Roman women of the time of the Emperors, reclining upon couches in the antique style, rather than Frenchwomen of less than one hundred years ago. Such however was the costume of the beauties of the salons of the Directory, those fair Parisians who crowded round Garat while he sang his ' romances,' or danced the gavotte, or the waltz, then the very newest novelty, with the handsome Trénitz.

In 1803, or 1804, the 'Titus' style of hairdressing had ceased to be fashionable, it was 'old,' it was 'provincial.' And what of the hair that was not to be hurried into growing long again, immediately upon the change of taste? The ladies bemoaned their luxuriant locks, fair, brown, or auburn, and were obliged

PREMIER EMPIRE.

to have recourse to 'fronts' in order to display ringlets once more, and to make up their Etruscan chignons with borrowed plaits.

It was an unfortunate moment for feminine costume. Fashion itself seemed to have been conquered by the great conqueror, and to have devoted all the zeal and grace of its fancy to dressing magnificently, braiding, embroidering, gilding, and befeathering the innumerable squadrons of gallant swordsmen about to be despatched by His Majesty the Emperor and King to gallop all over Europe, and to be flung upon the cannon and the bayonets of its united peoples.

What, we may ask, did the Frascati Salons and the Tivoli Gardens, whither the fair ladies of the Directory in their bold undress, in their transparent tunics, and all their Athenian frippery, had resorted, think of the costumes now worn by these very same women, or by their younger sisters?

What did they think of the ugly bags which were called gowns, of the ridiculous 'sheaths,' the lamp-shade hats, and the cabriolet-hood bonnets?

Masculine fashions were no less inelegant. Let those who would not consent to adopt them enlist in the Hussars! The ugliness of male costume, which increased in the course of the century, had already set in.

But the women!—Here is a fine lady of 1810!

First, the skirt—there is so little bodice that the skirt forms almost the whole costume—is of print or some common stuff; it begins under the arms, hangs ungracefully down to the feet, or is cut short just over the tops of the boots; a few folds, four or five rows of notched trimming, or three little flounces, form its sole ornament. The bodice is hardly perceptible, a tight girdle is placed close under the bosom; for sleeves there are two thick rolls at the shoulders, which are also bared, and this hideous dress is finished off by a worked muslin tippet, or a big collar made of several rows of quilled net. The latter were the only possibly pretty features of the toilette, but even these were put on so ungracefully that they were cumbersome rather than ornamental.

Beginning of the 19th century.

Hats and bonnets were mostly ridiculous. As all heads were full of the army and war, the ladies stuck head-gear of extraordinary shapes atop of their senseless costumes; some-

times a kind of helmet, with a wreath and a
great tuft of feathers, sometimes a big hat in
the form of a shako, and even real helmets
were worn, and named *à la Clorinde*, in
memory of those of the Knights-Crusaders.

For a while small caps were the mode; these
were just like infant's caps trimmed with lace,
and gave the wearers a pretty childlike air.
But the triumph of the period was the
big 'cabriolet' hat, an enormous hood that
stretched out far beyond the face, which was
hidden in the depths of the ungainly structure.
Sometimes these 'cabriolets' boasted the
monstrous addition of a tube-shaped crown,
taller than the tallest shako in all His
Majesty's armies.

The women of those times needed to be
really handsome to captivate, in this hideous
head-gear, the brilliant officers who between
two victorious campaigns came to singe their
hearts, like moths' wings, at the flame of
bright eyes.

At balls and receptions, in the salons

where the gilded military butterflies threw humble civilians into the shade, the ladies, who no longer affected the triumphant airs of the 'Merveilleuses' of the preceding period, assumed a dove-like gentleness and timidity

Waiting for the conquerors.

beneath the gaze of the plumed heroes. Their ball-dresses had extremely short skirts adorned with bunches of flowers, showing the leg and the buskin, no longer the antique cothurnus of the fair Tallien, but a buskin-shoe, tied with ribbons upon the instep.

These belles of the Empire, these sentimental Malvinas in baggy gowns, who were dreaming of the gallant warriors beyond the Rhine, wore

Large Empire Hat.

their hair either piled into a helmet-shape, or 'à la Chinoise,' drawn tightly up on the top of the head.

Serious beauties assumed the turban of the Turk. Everybody knows the famous portrait of Mme. de Staël in her imposing turban. The salons were crowded with Parisian Odalisques, and their head-dress was pro-

Oriental Dress and Turban.

nounced charming. After this, what is there that a pretty face and fine eyes, either lively or languorous, will not make acceptable?

Presently these turbans grew to a vast size, and were adorned with gauze scarfs of various colours, and feathers. Under the Restoration turbans became the special wear of mammas and mothers-in-law, and gave them so comic an aspect, that it is impossible to look at the portraits of the period without laughter.

And then, only to think of the 'Spencers,' the heavy 'Carricks,' or driving-coats, the furred 'top-coats,' and the 'Vitchouras!' Furs were very fashionable; astrakhan, marten, or sable was worn on garments of all sorts, and in pelisses of every shape.

All these queerly-dressed people, all those women whose costumes seem to be divided by ages from the attire of the eighteenth century, and also from the furbelows that their own mothers had worn, lived amid objects and surroundings entirely different from those of the recent 'rococo' period.

Are we in France or in Greece, in Egypt, in Etruria, or in Palmyra? In what century are we living, the nineteenth after or before the Christian era? The antique form, which was assumed all of a sudden, dates from the

PARISIENNE DE 1810.

Directory; it was introduced into Paris, and the hôtels of distinguished persons of fashion, by Percier and Fontaine, two architects who had returned from Rome, and was speedily adapted in the houses of the bourgeoisie.

Empire Hat.

Dress had become Greek and Roman; even before Percier and Fontaine exerted their influence, costume had preceded architecture this time, and assisted in the creation of a style.

Imagine the elegance of a salon which resembles a Greek temple, or recalls the interior of an Etruscan tomb! Chimney-pieces of funereal style, tripods copied from Pompeii, curule chairs, inconvenient arm-chairs,

Empire Head-dress.

adorned with lions, swans, and cornucopias, beds guarded by sphinxes, consoles laden with swords, couches in the forms of burial-litters, and altars, hard lines, stiff ornament-ation, and the everlasting palmetto, Greek or Etruscan borders, and afterwards, when the expedition to Egypt had brought the land of the Pharaohs into fashion, Egyptian designs.

One must have been blessed with large reserves of animal spirits to enjoy life in the midst of these hard, stiff shapes; daily life set in so solemn, antique, and stern a frame was calculated to produce a moodiness and ennui that were quite modern.

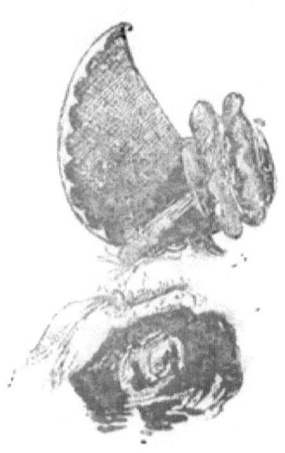

Hat worn in 1814.

XI.

THE RESTORATION AND THE JULY MONARCHY.

Full sleeves, and Leg-of-mutton sleeves—Collerettes—Giraffe fashions—Hair-dressing and big hats—1830—Expansion of 'Romantic' fashions—The last caps—1840—Chaste bands—Medium (Juste-milieu) fashions.

UNDER the Restoration the very ugly and inelegant fashions of the Empire were improved from year to year, and acquired some degree of gracefulness. Fashion had probably ceased to concentrate all its thoughts and all the resources of its genius upon the showy hussars and brilliant aides-de-camp of the French army. Feminine taste revived.

Costume was about to improve daily, to discard its commonplace stiffness, to enlarge its borders here, to make itself lighter there, and, from 1825, to become quite charming for the space of a decade.

Grace, distinction, originality, a supple and natural elegance, well-hung skirts, extremely becoming head-dresses, were among the delightful features of that period, and the women of 1830 have a right to a high place among the most charming figures of the past, when we evoke the dead modes of Yester-year.

At a later date, when our poor nineteenth century shall have slipped into the gulf which it is, alas, already approaching, when the belles of to-day shall have become grandmothers in their turn, when the typical women of our age come to be represented, those of 1830 will be chosen to represent its first, and those of 1890 its second half.

That was an epoch of good taste; the drawings and paintings of the time, by Devéria, Gavarni and others, bear witness to the graceful toilettes of the ladies from 1825 to 1835, from the second period of the Restoration to the early days of the July Monarchy, during the great renewal of ideas and arts.

Ah! We have known those women, and they are the most interesting of all to us, theirs are not vague faces summoned up from the far past. We have known them as good and charming old ladies, with curls around their faces as of yore; but the curls are white, the eyes which once were bright and laughing look through spectacles.

After the fall of the Empire, Anglo-mania in dress prevailed for some years, and also a touch of Cossacko-mania; Paris imported fashions from London, but by degrees this ceased to be the case, and the Mode at length began to invent very pretty styles.

The 'bag'-shaped gown and the sheath gown continued to be worn for a few years, with attempts at bodices, somewhat longer

Hat—1815.

waists, large puffed sleeves, and more or less ugly hats, of the oddest shapes, and great size; sometimes, indeed, the face was almost completely hidden.

With tranquillity, however, luxury revived. With the return of the Court, and a repose that had not been known for twenty-five years, the salons recovered their former brilliancy, and were no longer little gatherings whereat malcontents, or mere gossips, discussed the last victory or the last reverse of the Emperor, as the sole subject of conversation between two rubbers of whist. Let us take up one of the old slides of the great magic-lantern which time passes before us so rapidly, and we shall find the fine ladies of the Restoration, the romantic belles, and the 'lionnes' of the July Monarchy attired as follows.

The gown is white 'gros de Naples' with yellow flounces at the bottom of the widened skirt, the same trimming is worn on the shoulders in pelerine shape, the sleeves are 'leg-of-mutton'—the latter newly 'out,' and contemporaneous with the 'elephant' and 'imbecile' sleeves. With this gown is worn a

PARISIENNE 1814.

fluted collerette, and a big hat of rice-straw with satin ribbons and nodding feathers. We may

Evening-dress: Restoration period.

also observe fuller skirts, trimmed with gauze puffs and satin bows, lace flounces and inser-

Q

tion, canezous, tartan skirts, large decorative hats adorned with big bunches of flowers—Mme. Herbault's hats, worn by all the belles in the chronicles and novels of the period—and loose gloves completely covering the arms.

That lady who is dreamily playing the harp at a fashionable party, whose shoulders are draped in a scarf of striped gauze, wears on her head a large Scotch or Tam-o'-shanter cap (béret) which suits her poetic profile; on leaving the salon madame will wrap herself up in a cape, or in a fur-lined cloak made with a tippet and a large collar, while monsieur, in a curled toupee, a blue coat with brass buttons, and tights, will put on his box-coat.[1]

For summer wear, for the country, for walking, for visits to the Tivoli wizard, there are canezous of Organdy muslin ruched with tulle, and large straw hats with broad upstanding ribbons. For the theatre, and for outdoor wear in cold weather there are boas (these

[1] Carrick.

have recently been revived), which afforded opportunities for many pretty movements, as the serpents of fur were twined about bare shoulders, and also showed off the delicate tints of the complexion.

Hat—1820.

In 1827, in honour of the arrival of the first giraffe at the Jardin des Plantes, all the fashions were 'à la Girafe.'

In 1830, the sole remainder of the giraffe fashion was the large tortoiseshell comb which was worn at the top, crowning the edifice. The hair was dressed very high, in several bows, with curls falling irregularly, three on one side, four on the other, around the face. The fashionable fair of 1830 was a charming person in her evening dress, with the completely developed leg-of-mutton sleeve, her shoulders emerging from a line of fine lace, the nape of her neck fully shown under the large comb fixed in the fair or dark tresses, which were drawn up and gathered together at the top of her head. In the street, on the boulevards at the promenades, or in the Champs-Élysées, she still wore a low-necked gown, and draped, but did not hide herself in a little shawl coquettishly adjusted.

Let us return for awhile to the subject of head-dresses, which is not without importance. The head-dresses of the period may be classified as chivalric and Ossianic, toques and Tam-o'-shanters (bérets), caps and turbans, and finally, hats.

It would need a poet fitly to extol the

grandeur, and bewail the decline of the feminine hat. Under the Restoration, until 1835, the hat was in its glorious and triumphant period, it rested proudly on the head, it

A gauze 'beret.'

flaunted its plumes, with gracefully swaying bows, and big satin knots. After the disfiguring 'blunderbuss' or shako of the Empire—a mere tube enclosing the face at the end of a dark passage—the hat underwent alterations, it was widened and opened. Formerly it had been set quite straight upon the head, now it was daintily placed sideways upon the hair, which was rolled into large irregular curls. The nape of the neck was most becomingly displayed, the shoulders were also seen under the shade of a big hat, for bodices were worn very low-necked, and were not invariably edged with a fluted collerette.

This was the hour of triumph for the hat, but its decline was coming fast; the turned-up brim, horn-shaped, or in a long roll, was about to reappear, ribbons and plumes were to be suppressed, the face was once more to be hidden at the end of the passage, and the neck to be concealed by a big ugly cottage-bonnet. And from that time forth we were to have a whole series of lamentable inventions in eccentric and inelegant styles, even to the 'bibi' bonnet of the second Empire, and the ridiculous 'plate' hat of 1867.

But a reaction has set in, of late years we

have seen some really pretty and becoming hats and bonnets.

Large Restoration Hat.

As for the cap, the ladies of those days wore, when at home, coquettish 'rumpled' caps, as big as hats, with a crown raised very high to hold the tall comb, and bordered with a quantity of lace and ribbon, which confined their curls, or 'English' ringlets. These were the last days of elegance in caps; henceforth the pretty cap was no more to be seen except in the country, for so long as the majestic 'hennins' of the Norman, or the various winged coifs of the Breton women shall last. After the pretty house-caps worn by the 'lionnes' of 1830, the decline of the cap set in. The capriciously-quilled cap looked well on the heads of milliners' girls and grisettes, with their pert, Parisian noses, and knowing, mocking eyes; it was still pretty, and, besides, it was the head-dress that they so lightly toss metaphorically over the highest windmills, but the cap of the grisette afterwards became the ungraceful head-dress worn by fat shopwomen, and it finally fell to the lowest level, that of the porteress.

The belle of 1830 went forth to conquest in the boudoirs of the Chaussée d'Antin, or on the

UNE ÉLÉGANTE AUX CHAMPS-ELYSÉES, RESTAURATION.

fashionable promenades—the Champs-Elysées or Longchamps—and she captured the hearts of dandies cramped in their high-collared coats,

House-cap.

as a sprightly, elegant person in wide, undulating skirts, and leg-of-mutton sleeves.

She could hide herself behind under the

brim of her big hat bristling with ribbons
and feathers, by a mere movement of the
neck, securing a strict incognito. When she
rode in the Bois de Boulogne she wore a
coloured habit with leg-of-mutton sleeves,
adorned with frogs, or 'Brandenburgs,' or even
brightened up by a white canezou.

Unfortunately, she actually ventured at a
later date, when on horseback in the country,
to substitute the peaked cap, that hideous
'casquette' which is the disgrace of the nineteenth century, for her large hat with its graceful floating veil.

At this period numbers of pretty, bare-
necked women were to be seen at the fashionable theatres, in bodices opening in a peak
down to the waist over a wide, worked
chemisette, the trimmings of the bodice coming
up on the shoulders and sleeves. They also
wore looped boas, curls and 'heart-breakers'[1]
(inelegantly called spit-curls in England), and
had their hair dressed in several different and

[1] Accroche-cœurs.

complicated ways, with flowers, combs, and sprigs of satin.

Belles of the romantic school tried to outdo one another in mediæval toilettes. They sought

Riding-habit in 1830.

their literary pabulum in the Middle-Ages— the troubadours of the Vicomte d'Arlincourt, Ossian, Byron, and Walter Scott, had had their day—in the impassioned tirades of the great dramas of the time, *Hernani*, *La Tour de*

Nesle, and *Lucrèce Borgia*, and in the verses, novels, and chronicles of the 'romantic' writers of young France.

But, even on the stage, the Middle Ages were a good deal like 1830, for notwith-

Head-dress à la Chinoise, 1830.

standing the pains taken to reproduce local colouring, the heroines of those dramas, Isabeau, Marguerite de Bourgogne, or la Belle Ferronière, wore the inevitable leg-of-mutton sleeves, in common with the fair spectators, and, in reality, the belles of 1830, while trying hard to be mediaeval, were still up to date.

Alas! these pretty, graceful, feathery fashions,

Large hat and collerette.

of a 'truculent,' elegance, to employ an expression of the time, passed away. The antipicturesque bourgeois reaction, which set in with the Arts, achieved a far more rapid triumph

in dress. After a few years fashion became
—must the word be said?—wiser. In 1835 or
1836, fashion, the poetic, the romantic, the
chivalric, became commonplace, the fashion of
shopkeepers and the wives of the National
Guard! In 1835, fashion discarded grace, and
adopted clumsiness, by exaggerating the characteristics of 1830. The women were no longer
those of Devéria and Gavarni, they are those
of Grandville.

Skirts were as big as bells, and untrimmed,
made either of plain white muslin, or printed
in silly little patterns like the wall-paper of the
same period. Big leg-of-mutton sleeves were
worn quite limp, hanging loose and low over
narrow wristbands; over the bodice were large
worked pelerines edged with lace, and falling
below the waist. Add to this a large bonnet
of Leghorn or rice-straw, closed and tied under
the chin, and the combination is certainly not
attractive.

Contemplating the ladies of 1830 ten years
later, in 1840, we find them wearing shape-

less, untrimmed skirts, hesitating sleeves which retain just enough of the fullness of the leg-of-mutton to be ugly, 'anyhow' bodices, and

House dress.

unsightly bonnets tied under the chin by unsightly ribbons.

Hair-dressing has none of the pretty audacity of former times; flat bands make a cold, hard framework for the face, those 'chaste' bands, as they were then called, which killed all grace, and all beauty; there were also the 'English' ringlets, drooping like the twigs of the weeping-

Romantic dress.

willow, and giving a whimpering expression to the most cheerful of feminine faces. Fashion became more and more dull and ugly at the end of the July Monarchy. Taste there was

TOILETTES D'INTÉRIEUR 1830.

none; insipidity and commonplace were supreme.

The fashions always go from the widest to the narrowest, and come back from the narrowest to the widest. This is a law. It

1830.

is the same in the case of head-gear, the mode goes, and always will go, from the smallest to the largest, and back again from the largest to the smallest, with unfailing regularity.

After the panier of the time of Louis XV.

and Louis XVI. came the clinging gown of the Directory—the primitive expression of the skirt—and then nothing remained but its suppression. From the 'sheath' gowns of the Empire, amplitude was developed by degrees, and the great maximum of width was regained under the Second Empire, with the third restoration of the farthingale, now bearing the name of crinoline.

1835.

1845.

XII.

THE MODERN EPOCH.

1848—Revolutions everywhere, except in the kingdom of Fashion—Universal reign of crinoline—Cashmere shawls—The Talma, the burnous, and the 'pinch-waist' (pince-taille) — Sea-side fashions — Short gowns—The 'jump in' costume (saute-en-barque)—Wide and narrow skirts—Clinging fashions—Poufs and bustles—Valois fashions—More erudition than imagination—A 'fin-de-siècle' fashion in demand.

THE Revolution of 1848, unlike the first, did not affect Fashion at all; it did not drive the mode into new paths. In that day of topsy-turveydom, when the whole of Europe seemed to be infected by the revolutionary spirit, when the excited brain of the nations was crowded with many dreams, more or less fair, more or less foolish, fashion, which may certainly be admitted to be mad nor'-nor'-west, conducted itself with wisdom and prudence; indeed it remained so distinctly bourgeois that it might have been supposed to be 'set' by Mme. Prudhomme. Mean and ugly bonnets of a smaller 'cabriolet' kind, tied under the chin with narrow ribbons, were universally worn; in fact only one shape, with the curtain, and ribbon-trimming, was in vogue. Gowns, too, were quite plain, the bodice very long, the skirt straight.

With these flat dresses, shawls and small mantles were worn. Such was the sober and retiring toilette of the beginning of the Second Empire, a régime destined to transform it by degrees into a complicated, showy, and exaggerated costume, of doubtful taste and no style, with the exception, about 1864, of a few passing alterations and additions.

The main idea of the reign—so far as fashion was concerned—the great innovation which was to give the tone to toilette, was Crinoline, hooted, attacked, contemned by journalists, caricaturists, husbands, everybody, but victorious over all the clamour and all the mockery,

Bonnet, 1848.

as well as over the blame which it really deserved.

It may be said quite truly that under the Empire woman occupied three or four times as much place in the world—at least in circumference—as during any preceding period, even that of Louis XV. of unvirtuous memory, for crinoline reigned more despotically than paniers. It was adopted by women of every class, and girls who worked in the fields did not consider themselves dressed on Sundays unless they wore balloon-shaped steel hoops like those of the town ladies.

Bustles, and petticoats flounced with horsehair stuff, had made the eye gradually familiar with the enlargement of skirts, and when crinoline, pure and simple, was abandoned, first for steel hoops, and then for the 'cage' with hoops and cross-bars of steel, the ladies were delighted with the balloon-like effect, and the cage-crinoline became fashionable all over the world.

It is unnecessary to dwell upon the many objections to this mode—we can remember what they were—or upon its inconvenience; but, from the æsthetic point of view, crinoline ought to be solemnly anathematized, ridiculed, and excommunicated, for ever—that is to say until the day of its re-appearance under another name.

It is true that the skirts which were spread out over the much-reviled crinolines looked like wobbling domes, and that the entire

Crinoline.

toilette was loaded in a heavy and awkward style with little shabby adjuncts applied to common stuffs, while the paniers of the eighteenth century were worn under the artistically-trimmed skirts of gowns made of rich brocade and flowered stuffs. The exaggeration and the absurdity of paniers possessed the charm of gracefulness, while crinoline had nothing to redeem its ridiculous movement. The masterpiece of Imperial fashion was overdone.

With these absurd and intrusive crinolines, worn by the women of the period, we may recall the memory of the Talma, the burnous, a rather pretty Algerian mantle, the 'pinch-waist' in ribbed silk with pagoda sleeves—oh! that pagoda sleeve! It was an ugly and inconvenient funnel made uglier by lace or fringe trimming.

Special mention must be made of shawls, the famous Indian cashmere, and the large 'tapis' shawl. The elegance of the shawl has been much lauded, but in fact it is not elegant at all, unless it be small, almost as narrow as a scarf, and worn with an easy carelessness. What is there to be said for the big shawl, hitched upon its wearer's shoulders as though

PARISIENNE 1835.

upon a clothes' peg, and hanging straight down, hiding her figure and her attire? Merely that it is an ugly garment, and fit only to be worn by market-women on Sundays.

Among convenient inventions we may notice capelines, zouave jackets, red garibaldis, and

Second Empire Bonnet.

figaros, among the commendable novelties of the Empire.

Bonnets were not meritorious. About 1863, the cabriolet shape, with a curtain, and flowers both outside and inside the brim, was universally worn; it was in fact only the original big bonnet of the Restoration period, spoiled, ridiculously trimmed, and coming to a lamentable end.

Such, then, was the unbounded luxury with which President Dupin reproached the women of the time, in the famous pamphlet that made a sensation in 1865,—the luxury which attained its utmost height in the great City on Grand-Prix days, spreading from the hippodrome of Longchamps all along the boulevards, the luxury which, we were told, made of Paris a second Byzantium in decline, gave scandal to the worthy bourgeoise in a little shawl, and brought blushes to the cheeks of the rest of virtuous Europe, still constant to sweet simplicity, and practising the cult of Saint Muslin at sixpence a yard.

This demoralizing and appalling luxury may have been unbounded, but it was not artistic, or in good taste, and it conveyed at great cost the impression of a sham.

Although the recoil has not yet gone far enough to enable us to estimate or pass judgment upon the fashions of the Second-Empire period as a whole, without being influenced by the sense of something ridiculous

that is always conveyed by things merely
'gone out,' it seems to me that the women
and the artists of the next century will regard
it very much as we do now. We cannot
imagine the painters of that future day reviving
the fashions of 1860 in their pictures, for the

Pinch-waist.[1]

delight of fine ladies and Americans in the
twentieth century.

Nevertheless, as the custom of sea-bathing
became more and more diffused, and was about
to develop into a regular annual migration of
the whole of the middle classes to the Norman

[1] Pince-taille.

or Breton coasts, these habitual summer excursions brought about some welcome changes in fashion.

In 1864, short dresses had a brief triumph, which originated at the fashionable sea-bathing places. No more trailing skirts, or long gowns with broad flounces were worn. The crinoline was retained, but moderated in its width, and skirts were draped, caught up, and adorned with a great variety of ornamental trimmings, all large and effective.

Fancy, which had been suppressed since 1830, was once more allowed some play. The very smart short skirts displayed very smart and much-adorned boots; thin little boots were these, coming well up above the ankle, and with high clinking heels. For a short time some fine ladies adopted the tall Louis Treize cane at the seaside.

To this period wide handsome mantles with large sleeves, and also the outdoor garment called 'jump-in' (Saute-en-barque) belong. Hats, quite different from the formal tied bonnet, and saucily perched a little on one side, like bull-fighters' hats,[1] with big tufts, or feathers, were worn. The hair was dressed low,

Large Empire mantle.

waved on the forehead, and placed in a long net at the back of the head.

Short skirts, which suited the crinolines so

[1] Known in England as the 'pork-pie.'

well, with broad belts and buckles, and all the braid and gimp with which fashionable costume was covered, were, however, speedily displaced by a return to the objectionable long dresses, and fashion immediately lost its smartness.

The crinoline itself was eclipsed for a while, in 1867, when flat, trained gowns, and 'peplum' bodices (denoting a revival of the taste for tragedy—fragments from the great French tragedies were recited at this time at the Café-Concert), little 'plate' bonnets stuck on in front of the big ball-like chignons, with streamers down the back, called by the expressive name of "Follow me, young man!" became popular. And so the fight between wide skirts and narrow skirts went on; crinoline, having held out for a few years, was finally beaten and dead. The big-hooped crinoline now belongs to the domain of archæology; it is an antique, like the panier and the farthingale.

As width was still desired, the defeated petticoat was succeeded by the 'pouf,' a big bunch of the gown-material tucked up at the back over the skirt. Fashion was now on the path of anti-crinoline reaction, and the width of skirts was reduced and reduced, until at last gowns were actually moulded on the body, a mode which lasted two or three years, about 1880.[1] The fashions of that time were very pretty, very æsthetic; but after a while the least little increase of width was admitted, and soon after came the 'tournure,' or petticoat-bustle.

From the period of 'clinging' gowns, we still retain the jersey bodices, which mould the bust and the hips very becomingly. The jersey is admirably adapted to walking and country costume. For several summers, from one end of Europe to the other, on every beach in England, France, and elsewhere, the jersey was worn as a kind of obligatory uniform; women, young girls, children, boys or girls, all were dressed in dark blue jerseys, ornamented with gold anchors—every costume was a sailor's. Children still wear this becoming

[1] 'Tied-back' time in England.

and convenient garment, and now it is being adopted by tourists and cyclists.

The day of sumptuary edicts, and legislation by governments with the object of restraining luxury, is over. From the time of Philip the Fair to that of Richelieu a long series of edicts were issued; these were always rigorously applied just at first, before they fell into oblivion, even by kings who exhausted their Treasuries by the extravagance of their Courts. An instance of this is afforded by the bedizened fop, Henry III., who, in one of his fits of repression of other people's lavishness, threw thirty women into the prison of Fort l'Evêque in one day—and they not the least among Parisian ladies—for having defied his prohibition of brocade and silk.

The time of sumptuary prohibitions, of royal rescripts is over. In the general interests of industry and commerce, all that can develop luxury on a large scale must now be fostered. Luxury on a small scale ought, on the contrary, to be repressed as much as possible, or

MODES DE PLAGE 1864.

rather, it ought to have been repressed; the evil was wrought in past times, and it is now past remedy.

Clinging gown before 1880.

Ah! if fashion, which is mightier than kings and ministers, than decrees, laws, and edicts, had but ordained the preservation of the old feminine costumes of our provinces, the local modes which were in many instances so graceful and becoming, those rural refinements which Paris has so often borrowed, in the various forms of gowns, mantles, and head-dresses, the Bressan coifs, the lace caps of Caux, the large Breton coifs, the caps of the women of Arles, &c., &c., what a salvage there would have been!

But fashion did nothing of the kind, and those pretty things have vanished before the influx of sham and shabby finery, the tasteless caricature of Parisian elegance, in the shapeless 'confections' turned out by hundreds, and conveyed into the remotest parts of the country!

Local fashions, and the peculiar individual grace of dress that belongs to special regions, have finally ceded their place to new fashions which are mostly pretentious and ridiculous. The 'costume of the country' has vanished from all our provinces; it is lost, and now it is for 'the fashion of the towns' to indemnify us for the loss by some real grace and elegance.

Fashion is in a period of transition and experiment; for lack of new novelties, it is trying imitations of the novelties of the past—those which have grown old *enough*, as the Empress Joséphine's dressmaker said.

Valois Period.

Fashion goes from the Louis-Seize or Empire 'cut' to the attire of the Valois, to Louis-Treize bodices, to mediæval sleeves, or else to the leg-of-mutton sleeves of 1830. We shall see what will come of these experiments, and whether, in the case of the art of dress as in that of every other art, the study of the ancient shall bring forth the new.

Let us hope that an original fashion, 'fin de siècle,' to use the current phrase, may at last arise. If this be so, the granddaughters of the fair ladies of the present day will be able to form mental pictures of their grandmothers in attire that was really their own, a personal possession, and not in costumes borrowed from all the ages.

APPENDIX.

BALLADE

DES MODES DU TEMPS JADIS.

Du tout premier Vertugadin,
Celui qu'inventa Madame Eve
A celui qu'admirons soudain,
Que d'autres passant comme rêve !
Combien leur existence est brève !
Tu resplendis toujours pourtant,
O beauté changeante sans trêve,
Mais où sont les modes d'antan.

Où donc es-tu, riche bliaut
Armorié sur chaque maille,
Et le peliçon d'Isabeau ?
Escoffion de haute taille
Pour qui l'on vit mainte chamaille,
Hennin qui charma Buridan ?
Hélas, ce n'est plus qu'antiquaille--
Mais où sont les modes d'antan !

Où est la fraise de Margot,
Et le surcot doublé d'hermine,
Où sont les manches à gigot !
Habit cavalier d'héroïne
Que portait Reine ou baladine,
Large panier pompadourant,
Et toi-même aussi, crinoline—
Mais où sont les modes d'antan !

Envoi.

Dame, il ne fut point de semaine
Depuis le temps d'Eve pourtant
Qui n'eût caprices par trentaine.
Mais où sont les modes d'antan !

NOTES.

HEAD-GEAR, ETC. See p. 168.

The following lines bear witness, among other matters, to the height of the head-gear in England at this time.

"The buckle then its modest limits knew,
Now, like the ocean, dreadful to the view,
Hath broke its bounds, and swallowed up the shoe :
The wearer's foot, like his once fine estate,
Is almost lost, the encumbrance is so great.
Ladies may smile—are they not in the plot ?
The bounds of nature have not they forgot ?
Were they design'd to be, when put together,
Made up, like shuttlecocks, of cork and feather ?
Their pale-faced grandmammas appeared with grace
When dawning blushes rose upon the face ;
No blushes now their once-loved station seek ;
The foe is in possession of the cheek !
No heads of old, too high in feather'd state,
Hinder'd the fair to pass the lowest gate ;
A church to enter now, they must be bent,
If ever they should try the experiment."

    Prologue to Sheridan's *Trip to Scarborough*, acted in 1777.

CADOGAN. See p. 179.

For the Cadogan (said to be derived from the first Earl of Cadogan, who died in 1726), see *Murray's Dictionary*. The following quotation is given from *Memoirs of Baroness D'Oberkirch*, vol. ii. chap. ix.—"The Duchess of Bourbon had introduced at the Court of Montbéliard [the fashion] of Cadogans, hitherto worn only by gentlemen." It was a mode of plaiting and looping the hair behind, and has been revived of late years in Paris.

GUILLOTINE. See p. 203.

The guillotine at this time was canonized as "La Sainte Guillotine," and worn on necklaces in place of the cross.

Richard Clay & Sons, Limited, London & Bungay.

St. Dunstan's House, Fetter Lane,
London, E.C. 1892.

Select List of Books in all Departments of Literature

PUBLISHED BY

Sampson Low, Marston & Company, Ld.

ABBEY and PARSONS, *Quiet Life*, from drawings; motive by Austin Dobson, 31s. 6d.

ABBOTT, CHARLES C., *Waste Land Wanderings*, 10s. 6d.

ABERDEEN, EARL OF. See Prime Ministers.

ABNEY, CAPT., *Thebes and its Greater Temples*, 40 photos. 63s.

—— and CUNNINGHAM, *Pioneers of the Alps*, new ed. 21s.

About in the World. See Gentle Life Series.

—— *Some Fellows*, from my note-book, by "an Eton boy," 2s. 6d.; new edit. 1s.

ADAMS, CHARLES K., *Historical Literature*, 12s. 6d.

ADDISON, *Sir Roger de Coverley*, from the "Spectator," 6s.

AGASSIZ, ALEX., *Three Cruises of the "Blake,"* illust. 2 vols. 42s.

ALBERT, PRINCE. See Bayard Series.

ALCOTT, L. M. *Jo's Boys*, a sequel to "Little Men," 5s.

—— *Life, Letters and Journals*, by Ednah D. Cheney, 6s.

—— *Lulu's Library*, a story for girls, 3s. 6d.

—— *Old-fashioned Thanksgiving Day*, 3s. 6d.

—— *Proverb Stories*, 3s. 6d.

ALCOTT, L. M., *Recollections of my Childhood's Days*, 3s. 6d.

—— *Silver Pitchers*, 3s. 6d.

—— *Spinning-wheel Stories*, 5s.

—— See also Low's Standard Series and Rose Library.

ALDAM, W. H., *Flies and Fly-making*, with actual specimens on cardboard, 63s.

ALDEN, W. L. See Low's Standard Series.

ALFORD, LADY MARIAN, *Needlework as Art*, 21s.; l. p. 84s.

ALGER, J. G., *Englishmen in the French Revolution*, 7s. 6d.

Amateur Angler in Dove Dale, a three weeks' holiday, by E. M. 1s. 6d., 1s. and 5s.

ANDERSEN, H. C., *Fairy Tales*, illust. in colour by E. V. B. 25s., new edit. 5s.

—— *Fairy Tales*, illust. by Scandinavian artists, 6s.

ANDERSON, W., *Pictorial Arts of Japan*, 4 parts, 168s.; artist's proofs, 252s.

ANDRES, *Varnishes, Lacquers, Siccatives, & Sealing-wax*, 12s. 6d.

Angler's strange Experiences, by Cotswold Isys, new edit., 3s. 6d.

ANNESLEY, C., *Standard Opera Glass*, the plots of eighty operas, 3rd edit., 2s. 6d.

Annual American Catalogue of Books, 1886-89, each 10s. 6d., half morocco, 14s.

—— 1890, cloth, 15s., half morocco, cloth sides, 18s.

Antipodean Notes; a nine months' tour, by Wanderer, 7s. 6d.

APPLETON, *European Guide*, new edit., 2 parts, 10s. each.

ARCHER, W., *English Dramatists of To-day*, 8s. 6d.

ARLOT'S *Coach Painting*, from the French by A. A. Fesquet, 6s.

ARMYTAGE, Hon. Mrs., *Wars of Queen Victoria's Reign*, 5s.

ARNOLD, E., *Birthday Book;* by Kath. L. and Constance Arnold, 4s. 6d.

—— E. L. L., *Summer Holiday in Scandinavia*, 10s. 6d.

—— *On the Indian Hills, Coffee Planting, &c.*, 2 vols. 21s.

—— R., *Ammonia and Ammonium Compounds*, illust. 5s.

Artistic Japan, text, woodcuts, and coloured plates, vols. I.-VI., 15s. each.

ASBJÖRNSEN, P. C., *Round the Yule Log*, 7s. 6d.; new edit. 5s.

ASHE, R. P., *Two Kings of Uganda;* six years in Eastern Equatorial Africa, 6s.; new edit. 3s. 6d.

—— *Uganda, England's latest Charge*, stiff cover, 1s.

ASHTON, F. T., *Designing fancy Cotton and Woollen Cloths*, illust. 50s.

ATCHISON, C. C., *Winter Cruise in Summer Seas;* "how I found" health, 16s.

ATKINSON, J. B. *Overbeck.* See Great Artists.

ATTWELL, *Italian Masters*, especially in the National Gallery, 3s. 6d.

AUDSLEY, G. A., *Chromolithography*, 44 coloured plates and text, 63s.

—— *Ornamental Arts of Japan*, 2 vols. morocco, 23l. 2s.; four parts, 15l. 15s.

—— W. and G. A., *Ornament in all Styles*, 31s. 6d.

AUERBACH, B., *Brigitta* (B. Tauchnitz), 2s.; sewed, 1s. 6d.

—— *On the Height* (B. Tauchnitz), 3 vols. 6s.; sewed, 4s. 6d.

—— *Spinoza* (B. Tauchnitz), 2 vols. 4s.

AUSTRALIA. See F. Countries.

AUSTRIA. See F. Countries.

Autumn Cruise in the Ægean, by one of the party. See "Fitzpatrick."

BACH. See Great Musicians.

BACON. See English Philosophers.

—— DELIA, *Biography*, 10s. 6d.

BADDELEY, W. ST. CLAIR, *Love's Vintage;* sonnets and lyrics, 5s.

—— *Tchay and Chianti*, a short visit to Russia and Finland, 5s.

—— *Travel-tide*, 7s. 6d.

BAKER, JAMES, *John Westacott*, new edit. 6s. and 3s. 6d.

BALDWIN, J., *Story of Siegfried*, illust. 6s.

—— *Story of Roland*, illust. 6s.

—— *Story of the Golden Age*, illust. 6s.

—— J. D., *Ancient America*, illust. 10s. 6d.

Ballad Stories. See Bayard Series.

Ballads of the Cid, edited by Rev. Gerrard Lewis, 3s. 6d.

BALLANTYNE, T., *Essays.* See Bayard Series.

In all Departments of Literature.

BALLIN, ADA S., *Science of Dress*, illust. 6s.
BAMFORD, A. J., *Turbans and Tails*, 7s. 6d.
BANCROFT, G., *History of America*, new edit. 6 vols. 73s. 6d.
Barbizon Painters, by J. W. Mollett—I. Millet, T. Rousseau, and Diaz, 3s. 6d. II. Corot, Daubigny and Dupré, 3s. 6d.; the two in one vol. 7s. 6d.
BARING-GOULD. See Foreign Countries.
BARLOW, A., *Weaving*, new edit. 25s.
—— P. W., *Kaipara, New Z.*, 6s.
—— W., *Matter and Force*, 12s.
BARRETT. See Gr. Musicians.
BARROW, J., *Mountain Ascents*, new edit. 5s.
BASSETT, *Legends of the Sea*, 7s. 6d.
BATHGATE, A., *Waitaruna, New Zealand*, 5s.
Bayard Series, edited by the late J. Hain Friswell; flexible cloth extra, 2s. 6d. each.
Chevalier Bayard, by Berville.
De Joinville, St. Louis.
Essays of Cowley.
Abdallah, by Laboullaye.
Table-Talk of Napoleon.
Vathek, by Beckford.
Cavalier and Puritan Songs.
Words of Wellington.
Johnson's Rasselas.
Hazlitt's Round Table.
Browne's Religio Medici.
Ballad Stories of the Affections, by Robert Buchanan.
Coleridge's Christabel, &c.
Chesterfield's Letters.
Essays in Mosaic, by T. Ballantyne.
My Uncle Toby.
Rochefoucauld, Reflections.
Socrates, Memoirs from Xenophon.
Prince Albert's Precepts.

BEACONSFIELD, *Public Life*, 3s. 6d.
—— See also Prime Ministers.
BEAUGRAND, *Young Naturalists*, new edit. 5s.
BECKER, A.L., *First German Book*, 1s.; *Exercises*, 1s.; Key to both, 2s. 6d.; *German Idioms*, 1s. 6d.
BECKFORD. See Bayard Series.
BEECHER, H. W., *Biography*, new edit. 10s. 6d.
BEETHOVEN. See Great Musicians.
BEHNKE, E., *Child's Voice*, 3s. 6d.
BELL, *Obeah, Witchcraft in the West Indies*, 2s. 6d.
BELLENGER & WITCOMB'S *French and English Conversations*, new edit. Paris, bds. 2s.
BENJAMIN, *Atlantic Islands as health, &c., resorts*. 16s.
BERLIOZ. See Gr. Musicians.
BERVILLE. See Bayard Series.
BIART, *Young Naturalist*, new edit. 7s. 6d.
—— *Involuntary Voyage*, 7s. 6d. and 5s.
—— *Two Friends*, translated by Mary de Hauteville, 7s. 6d.
See also Low's Standard Books.
BICKERSTETH, ASHLEY, B.A., *Outlines of Roman History*, 2s. 6d.
—— E. H., Exon., *Clergyman in his Home*, 1s.
—— *From Year to Year*, original poetical pieces, morocco or calf, 10s. 6d.; padded roan, 6s.; roan, 5s.; cloth, 3s. 6d.
—— *Hymnal Companion*, full lists post free.
—— *Master's Home Call*, new edit. 1s.
—— *Octave of Hymns*, sewn, 3d., with music, 1s.

BICKERSTETH, E. H., Exon., *Reef, Parables,* &c., illust. 7s. 6d. and 2s. 6d.
—— *Shadowed Home,* n. ed. 5s.
BIGELOW, JOHN, *France and the Confederate Navy,* an international episode, 7s. 6d.
BILBROUGH, *'Twixt France and Spain,* 7s. 6d.
BILLROTH, *Care of the Sick,* 6s.
BIRD, F. J., *Dyer's Companion,* 42s.
—— F. S., *Land of Dykes and Windmills,* 12s. 6d.
—— H. E., *Chess Practice,* 2s. 6d.
BISHOP. See Nursing Record Series.
BLACK, ROBERT, *Horse Racing in France,* 14s.
—— W., *Donald Ross of Heimra,* 3 vols. 31s. 6d.
—— Novels, new and uniform edition in monthly vols. 2s. 6d. ea.
—— See Low's Standard Novels.
BLACKBURN, C. F., *Catalogue Titles, Index Entries,* &c. 14s.
—— H., *Art in the Mountains,* new edit. 5s.
—— *Artists and Arabs,* 7s. 6d.
—— *Breton Folk,* new issue, 10s. 6d.
—— *Harz Mountains,* 12s.
—— *Normandy Picturesque,* 16s.
—— *Pyrenees,* illust. by Gustave Doré, new edit. 7s. 6d.
BLACKMORE, R.D., *Georgics,* 4s. 6d.; cheap edit. 1s.
—— *Lorna Doone, édit. de luxe,* 35s., 31s. 6d. & 21s.
—— *Lorna Doone,* illust. by W. Small, 7s. 6d.
—— *Springhaven,* illust. 12s.; new edit. 7s. 6d. & 6s.
—— See also Low's Standard Novels.

BLAIKIE, *How to get Strong,* new edit. 5s.
—— *Sound Bodies for our Boys and Girls,* 2s. 6d.
BLOOMFIELD. See Choice Editions.
Bobby, a Story, by Vesper, 1s.
BOCK, *Head Hunters of Borneo,* 36s.
—— *Temples & Elephants,* 21s.
BONAPARTE, MAD. PATTERSON, *Life,* 10s. 6d.
BONWICK, JAMES, *Colonial Days,* 2s. 6d.
—— *Colonies,* 1s. ea.; 1 vol. 5s.
—— *Daily Life of the Tasmanians,* 12s. 6d.
—— *First Twenty Years of Australia,* 5s.
—— *Last of the Tasmanians,* 16s.
—— *Port Philip,* 21s.
—— *Lost Tasmanian Race,* 4s.
BOSANQUET, C., *Blossoms from the King's Garden,* 6s.
—— *Jehoshaphat,* 1s.
—— *Lenten Meditations,* I. 1s. 6d.; II. 2s.
—— *Tender Grass for Lambs,* 2s. 6d.
BOULTON, N. W. *Rebellions,* Canadian life, 9s.
BOURKE, *On the Border with Crook,* illust., roy. 8vo, 21s.
—— *Snake Dance of Arizona,* 21s.
BOUSSENARD. See Low's Standard Books.
BOWEN, F., *Modern Philosophy,* new ed. 16s.
BOWER. See English Philosophers.
—— *Law of Electric Lighting,* 12s. 6d.
BOYESEN, H. H., *Against Heavy Odds,* 5s.
—— *History of Norway,* 7s. 6d.

In all Departments of Literature. 5

BOYESEN, *Modern Vikings*, 6s.
Boy's Froissart, King Arthur, Mabinogian, Percy, see "Lanier."
BRADSHAW, *New Zealand as it is*, 12s. 6d.
—— *New Zealand of To-day*, 14s.
BRANNT, *Fats and Oils*, 35s.
—— *Soap and Candles*, 35s.
—— *Vinegar, Acetates*, 25s.
—— *Distillation of Alcohol*, 12s. 6d.
—— *Metal Worker's Receipts*, 12s. 6d.
—— *Metallic Alloys*, 12s. 6d.
—— and WAHL, *Techno-Chemical Receipt Book*, 10s. 6d.
BRASSEY, LADY, *Tahiti*, 21s.
BRÉMONT. See Low's Standard Novels.
BRETON, JULES, *Life of an Artist*, an autobiography, 7s. 6d.
BRISSE, *Menus and Recipes*, new edit. 5s.
Britons in Brittany, by G. H. F. 2s. 6d.
BROCK-ARNOLD. See Great Artists.
BROOKS, NOAH, *Boy Settlers*, 6s.
BROWN, A. J., *Rejected of Men*, 3s. 6d.
—— A. S. *Madeira and Canary Islands for Invalids*, 2s. 6d.
—— *Northern Atlantic*, for travellers, 4s. 6d.
—— ROBERT. See Low's Standard Novels.
BROWNE, LENNOX, and BEHNKE, *Voice, Song, & Speech*, 15s.; new edit. 5s.
—— *Voice Use*, 3s. 6d.
—— SIR T. See Bayard Series.
BRYCE, G., *Manitoba*, 7s. 6d.
—— *Short History of the Canadian People*, 7s. 6d.

BUCHANAN, R. See Bayard Series.
BULKELEY, OWEN T., *Lesser Antilles*, 2s. 6d.
BUNYAN. See Low's Standard Series.
BURDETT-COUTTS, *Brookfield Stud*, 5s.
BURGOYNE, *Operations in Egypt*, 5s.
BURNABY, F. See Low's Standard Library.
—— MRS., *High Alps in Winter*, 14s.
BURNLEY, JAMES, *History of Wool*, 21s.
BUTLER, COL. SIR W. F., *Campaign of the Cataracts*, 18s.
—— *Red Cloud*, 7s. 6d. & 5s.
—— See also Low's Standard Books.
BUXTON, ETHEL M. WILMOT, *Wee Folk*, 5s.
—— See also Illust Text Books.
BYNNER. See Low's Standard Novels.
CABLE, G. W., *Bonaventure*, 5s.
CADOGAN, LADY A., *Drawing-room Comedies*, illust. 10s. 6d., acting edit. 6d.
—— *Illustrated Games of Patience*, col. diagrams, 12s. 6d.
—— *New Games of Patience*, with coloured diagrams, 12s. 6d.
CAHUN. See Low's Standard Books.
CALDECOTT, RANDOLPH, *Memoir*, by H. Blackburn, new edit. 7s. 6d. and 5s.
—— *Sketches*, pict. bds. 2s. 6d.
CALL, ANNIE PAYSON, *Power through Repose*, 3s. 6d.
CALLAN, H., M.A., *Wanderings on Wheel and Foot through Europe*, 1s. 6d.
Cambridge Trifles, 2s. 6d.

Cambridge Staircase, 2s. 6d.
CAMPBELL, LADY COLIN, *Book of the Running Brook*, 5s.
—— T. See Choice Editions.
CANTERBURY, ARCHBISHOP. See Preachers.
CARLETON, WILL, *City Ballads*, illust. 12s. 6d.
—— *City Legends*, ill. 12s. 6d.
—— *Farm Festivals*, ill. 12s. 6d.
—— See also Rose Library.
CARLYLE, *Irish Journey in 1849*, 7s. 6d.
CARNEGIE, ANDREW, *American Four-in-hand in Britain*, 10s. 6d.; also 1s.
—— *Round the World*, 10s. 6d.
—— *Triumphant Democracy*, 6s.; new edit. 1s. 6d.; paper, 1s.
CAROVÉ, *Story without an End*, illust. by E. V. B., 7s. 6d.
Celebrated Racehorses, 4 vols. 126s.
CÉLIÈRE. See Low's Standard Books.
Changed Cross, &c., poems, 2s. 6d.
Chant-book Companion to the Common Prayer, 2s.; organ ed. 4s.
CHAPIN, *Mountaineering in Colorado*, 10s. 6d.
CHAPLIN, J. G., *Bookkeeping*, 2s. 6d.
CHATTOCK, *Notes on Etching* new edit. 10s. 6d.
CHERUBINI. See Great Musicians.
CHESTERFIELD. See Bayard Series.
Choice Editions of choice books, illustrated by C. W. Cope, R.A., T. Creswick, R.A., E. Duncan, Birket Foster, J. C. Horsley, A.R.A., G. Hicks, R. Redgrave, R.A., C. Stonehouse, F. Tayler, G. Thomas, H. G. Townsend,

Choice Editions—continued.
E. H. Wehnert, Harrison Weir, &c., cloth extra gilt, gilt edges, 2s. 6d. each; re-issue, 1s. each.
Bloomfield's Farmer's Boy.
Campbell's Pleasures of Hope.
Coleridge's Ancient Mariner.
Goldsmith's Deserted Village.
Goldsmith's Vicar of Wakefield.
Gray's Elegy in a Churchyard.
Keats' Eve of St. Agnes.
Milton's Allegro.
Poetry of Nature, by H. Weir.
Rogers' Pleasures of Memory.
Shakespeare's Songs and Sonnets.
Elizabethan Songs and Sonnets.
Tennyson's May Queen.
Wordsworth's Pastoral Poems.
CHREIMAN, *Physical Culture of Women*, 1s.
CLARK, A., *A Dark Place of the Earth*, 6s.
—— Mrs. K. M., *Southern Cross Fairy Tale*, 5s.
CLARKE, C. C., *Writers, and Letters*, 10s. 6d.
—— PERCY, *Three Diggers*, 6s.
—— *Valley Council;* from T. Bateman's Journal, 6s.
Classified Catalogue of English-printed Educational Works, 3rd edit. 6s.
Claude le Lorrain. See Great Artists.
CLOUGH, A. H., *Plutarch's Lives*, one vol. 18s.
COLERIDGE, C. R., *English Squire*, 6s.
—— S. T. See Choice Editions and Bayard Series.
COLLINGWOOD, H. See Low's Standard Books.
COLLINSON, Adm. SIR R., *H.M.S. Enterprise in Search of Franklin*, 14s.
CONDER, J., *Flowers of Japan; Decoration*, coloured Japanese Plates, 42s. nett.

CORREGGIO. See Great Artists.
COWLEY. See Bayard Series.
COX, DAVID. See Great Artists.
COZZENS, F., *American Yachts*, pfs. 21*l*.; art. pfs. 31*l*. 10*s*.
—— See also Low's Standard Books.
CRADDOCK. See Low's Standard Novels.
CREW, B. J., *Petroleum*, 21*s*.
CRISTIANI, R. S., *Soap and Candles*, 42*s*.
—— *Perfumery*, 25*s*.
CROKER, Mrs. B. M. See Low's Standard Novels.
CROUCH, A. P., *Glimpses of Feverland* (West Africa), 6*s*.
—— *On a Surf-bound Coast*, 7*s*. 6*d*.; new edit. 5*s*.
CRUIKSHANK, G. See Great Artists.
CUDWORTH, W., *Abraham Sharp*, 26*s*.
CUMBERLAND, STUART, *Thought-reader's Thoughts*, 10*s*. 6*d*.
—— See also Low's Standard Novels.
CUNDALL, F. See Great Artists.
—— J., *Shakespeare*, 3*s*. 6*d*., 5*s*. and 2*s*.
CURTIN, J., *Myths of the Russians*, 10*s*. 6*d*.
CURTIS, C. B., *Velazquez and Murillo*, with etchings, 31*s*. 6*d*. and 63*s*.
CUSHING, W., *Anonyms*, 2 vols. 52*s*. 6*d*.
—— *Initials and Pseudonyms*, 25*s*.; ser. II., 21*s*.
CUTCLIFFE, H. C., *Trout Fishing*, new edit. 3*s*. 6*d*.
DALY, MRS. D., *Digging, Squatting, &c., in N. S. Australia*, 12*s*.

D'ANVERS, N., *Architecture and Sculpture*, new edit. 5*s*.
—— *Elementary Art, Architecture, Sculpture, Painting*, new edit. 10*s*. 6*d*.
—— *Elementary History of Music*, 2*s*. 6*d*.
—— *Painting*, by F. Cundall, 6*s*.
DAUDET, A., *My Brother Jack*, 7*s*. 6*d*.; also 5*s*.
—— *Port Tarascon*, by H. James, 7*s*. 6*d*.; new edit. 5*s*.
DAVIES, C., *Modern Whist*, 4*s*.
DAVIS, C. T., *Bricks, Tiles, &c.*, new edit. 25*s*.
—— *Manufacture of Leather*, 52*s*. 6*d*.
—— *Manufacture of Paper*, 28*s*.
—— *Steam Boiler Incrustation*, 8*s*. 6*d*.
—— G. B., *International Law*, 10*s*. 6*d*.
DAWIDOWSKY, *Glue, Gelatine, &c.*, 12*s*. 6*d*.
Day of my Life, by an Eton boy, new edit. 2*s*. 6*d*.; also 1*s*.
DE JOINVILLE. See Bayard Series.
DE LEON, EDWIN, *Under the Stars and Under the Crescent*, 2 vols. 12*s*.; new edit. 6*s*.
DELLA ROBBIA. See Great Artists.
Denmark and Iceland. See Foreign Countries.
DENNETT, R. E., *Seven Years among the Fjort*, 7*s*. 6*d*.
DERRY (Bishop of). See Preachers.
DE WINT. See Great Artists.
DIGGLE, J. W., *Bishop Fraser's Lancashire Life*, new edit. 12*s*. 6*d*.; popular ed. 3*s*. 6*d*.
—— *Sermons for Daily Life*, 5*s*

DOBSON, Austin, *Hogarth*, with a bibliography, &c., of prints, illust. 24s.; l. paper 52s. 6d.
—— See also Great Artists.
DODGE, Mrs., *Hans Brinker, the Silver Skates*, new edit. 5s., 3s. 6d., 2s. 6d.; text only, 1s.
DONKIN, J. G., *Trooper and Redskin;* N. W. mounted police, Canada, 8s. 6d.
DONNELLY, Ignatius, *Atlantis, the Antediluvian World*, new edit. 12s. 6d.
—— *Cæsar's Column*, authorized edition, 3s. 6d.
—— *Doctor Huguet*, 3s. 6d.
—— *Great Cryptogram*, Bacon's Cipher in Shakespeare, 2 vols. 30s.
—— *Ragnarok: the Age of Fire and Gravel*, 12s. 6d.
DORE, Gustave, *Life and Reminiscences*, by Blanche Roosevelt, fully illust. 24s.
DOS PASSOS, J. R., *Law of Stockbrokers and Stock Exchanges*, 35s.
DOUDNEY, Sarah, *Godiva Durleigh*, 3 vols. 31s. 6d.
DOUGALL, J. D., *Shooting Appliances, Practice, &c.*, 10s. 6d.; new edit. 7s. 6d.
DOUGHTY, H. M., *Friesland Meres and the Netherlands*, new edit. illust. 10s. 6d.
DOVETON, F. B., *Poems and Snatches of Songs*, 5s.; new edit. 3s. 6d.
DU CHAILLU, Paul. See Low's Standard Books.
DUNCKLEY ("Verax.") See Prime Ministers.
DUNDERDALE, George, *Prairie and Bush*, 6s.
Dürer. See Great Artists.
DYKES, J. Oswald. See Preachers.

Echoes from the Heart, 3s. 6d.
EDEN, C. H. See Foreign Countries.
EDMONDS, C., *Poetry of the Anti-Jacobin*, new edit. 7s. 6d. and 21s.
Educational Catalogue. See Classified Catalogue.
EDWARDS, *American Steam Engineer*, 12s. 6d.
—— *Modern Locomotive Engines*, 12s. 6d.
—— *Steam Engineer's Guide*, 12s. 6d.
—— H. Sutherland. See Great Musicians.
—— M. B., *Dream of Millions, &c.*, 1s.
—— See Low's Standard Novels.
EGGLESTON, G. Cary, *Juggernaut*, 6s.
Egypt. See Foreign Countries.
Elizabethan Songs. See Choice Editions.
EMERSON, Dr. P. H., *East Coast Yarns*, 1s.
—— *English Idylls*, new ed. 2s.
—— *Naturalistic Photography*, new edit. 5s.
—— *Pictures of East Anglian Life;* plates and vignettes, 105s. and 147s.
—— and GOODALL, *Life on the Norfolk Broads*, plates, 126s. and 210s.
—— *Wild Life on a Tidal Water*, copper plates, ord. edit. 25s.; édit. de luxe, 63s.
—— R. W., by G. W. Cooke, 8s. 6d.
—— *Birthday Book*, 3s. 6d.
—— *In Concord*, a memoir, 7s. 6d.
English Catalogue, 1863-71, 42s.; 1872-80, 42s.; 1881-9, 52s. 6d.; 5s. yearly.

English Catalogue, Index vol. 1837-56, 26s.; 1856-76, 42s.; 1874-80, 18s.
—— Etchings, vol. v. 45s.; vi., 25s.; vii., 25s.; viii., 42s.
English Philosophers, edited by E. B. Ivan Müller, M.A., 3s. 6d. each.
Bacon, by Fowler.
Hamilton, by Monck.
Hartley and James Mill, by Bower.
Shaftesbury & Hutcheson; Fowler.
Adam Smith, by J. A. Farrer.
ERCKMANN-CHATRIAN. See Low's Standard Books.
ERICHSON, Life, by W. C. Church, 2 vols. 24s.
ESMARCH, F., Handbook of Surgery, 24s.
Essays on English Writers. See Gentle Life Series.
EVANS, G. E., Repentance of Magdalene Despar, &c., poems, 5s.
—— S. & F., Upper Ten, a story, 1s.
—— W. E., Songs of the Birds, n. ed. 6s.
EVELYN, J., An Inca Queen, 5s.
—— John, Life of Mrs. Godolphin, 7s. 6d.
EVES, C. W., West Indies, n. ed. 7s. 6d.
FAIRBAIRN, A. M. See Preachers.
Familiar Words. See Gentle Life Series.
FARINI, G. A., Kalahari Desert, 21s.
FARRAR, C. S., History of Sculpture, &c., 6s.
—— Maurice, Minnesota, 6s.
FAURIEL, Last Days of the Consulate, 10s. 6d.
FAY, T., Three Germanys, 2 vols. 35s.

FEILDEN, H. St. J., Some Public Schools, 2s. 6d.
—— Mrs., My African Home, 7s. 6d.
FENN, G. Manville. See Low's Standard Books.
FENNELL, J. G., Book of the Roach, n. ed. 2s.
FFORDE, B., Subaltern, Policeman, and the Little Girl. 1s.
—— Trotter, a Poona Mystery, 1s.
FIELD, Maunsell B., Memories, 10s. 6d.
FIELDS, James T., Memoirs, 12s. 6d.
—— Yesterdays with Authors, 16s.; also 10s. 6d.
Figure Painters of Holland. See Great Artists.
FINCK, Henry T., Pacific Coast Scenic Tour, 10s. 6d.
FITCH, Lucy. See Nursing Record Series, 1s.
FITZGERALD. See Foreign Countries.
—— Percy, Book Fancier, 5s. and 12s. 6d.
FITZPATRICK, T., Autumn Cruise in the Ægean, 10s. 6d
—— Transatlantic Holiday, 10s. 6d.
FLEMING, S., England and Canada, 6s.
Foreign Countries and British Colonies, descriptive handbooks edited by F. S. Pulling, M.A. Each volume is the work of a writer who has special acquaintance with the subject, 3s. 6d.
Australia, by Fitzgerald.
Austria-Hungary, by Kay.
Denmark and Iceland, by E. C. Otté.
Egypt, by S. L. Poole.
France, by Miss Roberts.
Germany, by L. Sergeant.
Greece, by S. Baring Gould.

Foreign Countries, &c.—cont.
Japan, by Mossman.
Peru, by R. Markham.
Russia, by Morfill.
Spain, by Webster.
Sweden and Norway, by Woods.
West Indies, by C. H. Eden.
FOREMAN, J., *Philippine Islands*, 21s.
FOTHERINGHAM, L. M., *Nyassaland*, 7s. 6d.
FOWLER, *Japan, China, and India*, 10s. 6d.
FRA ANGELICO. See Great Artists.
FRA BARTOLOMMEO, ALBERTINELLI, and ANDREA DEL SARTO. See Great Artists.
FRANC, MAUD JEANNE, *Beatrice Melton*, 4s.
—— *Emily's Choice*, n. ed. 5s.
—— *Golden Gifts*, 4s.
—— *Hall's Vineyard*, 4s.
—— *Into the Light*, 4s.
—— *John's Wife*, 4s.
—— *Little Mercy; for better, for worse*, 4s.
—— *Marian, a Tale*, n. ed. 5s.
—— *Master of Ralston*, 4s.
—— *Minnie's Mission, a Temperance Tale*, 4s.
—— *No longer a Child*, 4s.
—— *Silken Cords and Iron Fetters, a Tale*, 4s.
—— *Two Sides to Every Question*, 4s.
—— *Vermont Vale*, 5s.
A plainer edition is published at 2s. 6d.
France. See Foreign Countries.
FRANCIS, F., *War, Waves, and Wanderings*, 2 vols. 24s.
—— See also Low's Standard Series.
Frank's Ranche; or, My Holiday in the Rockies, n. ed. 5s.

FRANKEL, JULIUS, *Starch Glucose, &c.*, 18s.
FRASER, BISHOP, *Lancashire Life*, n. ed. 12s. 6d.; popular ed. 3s. 6d.
FREEMAN, J., *Melbourne Life, lights and shadows*, 6s.
FRENCH, F., *Home Fairies and Heart Flowers*, illust. 24s.
French and English Birthday Book, by Kate D. Clark, 7s. 6d.
French Revolution, Letters from Paris, translated, 10s. 6d.
Fresh Woods and Pastures New, by the Author of "An Angler's Days," 5s., 1s. 6d., 1s.
FRIEZE, *Duprè, Florentine Sculptor*, 7s. 6d.
FRISWELL, J. H. See Gentle Life Series.
Froissart for Boys, by Lanier, new ed. 7s. 6d.
FROUDE, J. A. See Prime Ministers.
Gainsborough and Constable. See Great Artists.
GASPARIN, *Sunny Fields and Shady Woods*, 6s.
GEFFCKEN, *British Empire*, 7s. 6d.
Generation of Judges, n. e. 7s.6d.
Gentle Life Series, edited by J. Hain Friswell, sm. 8vo. 6s. per vol.; calf extra, 10s. 6d. ea.; 16mo, 2s. 6d., except when price is given.
Gentle Life.
About in the World.
Like unto Christ.
Familiar Words, 6s.; also 3s. 6d.
Montaigne's Essays.
Sidney's Arcadia, 6s.
Gentle Life, second series.
Varia; readings, 10s. 6d.
Silent hour; essays.
Half-length Portraits.
Essays on English Writers.
Other People's Windows, 6s. & 2s. 6d.
A Man's Thoughts.

George Eliot, by G. W. Cooke, 10s. 6d.

Germany. See Foreign Countries.

GESSI, ROMOLO PASHA, *Seven Years in the Soudan*, 18s.

GHIBERTI & DONATELLO. See Great Artists.

GILES, E., *Australia Twice Traversed*, 1872-76, 2 vols. 30s.

GILL, J. See Low's Readers.

GILLESPIE, W. M., *Surveying*, n. ed. 21s.

Giotto, by Harry Quilter, illust. 15s.

—— See also Great Artists.

GIRDLESTONE, C., *Private Devotions*, 2s.

GLADSTONE. See Prime Ministers.

GLENELG, P., *Devil and the Doctor*, 1s.

GLOVER, R., *Light of the World*, n. ed., 2s. 6d.

GLÜCK. See Great Musicians.

Goethe's Faustus, in orig. rhyme, by Huth, 5s.

—— *Prosa*, by C. A. Buchheim (Low's German Series), 3s. 6d.

GOLDSMITH, O., *She Stoops to Conquer*, by Austin Dobson, illust. by E. A. Abbey, 84s.

—— See also Choice Editions.

GOOCH, FANNY C., *Mexicans*, 16s.

GOODALL, *Life and Landscape on the Norfolk Broads*, 126s. and 210s.

—— &EMERSON, *Pictures of East Anglian Life*, £5 5s. and £7 7s.

GOODMAN, E. J., *The Best Tour in Norway*, 6s.

—— N. & A., *Fen Skating*, 5s.

GOODYEAR, W. H., *Grammar of the Lotus, Ornament and Sun Worship*, 63s. nett.

GORDON, J. E. H., *Physical Treatise on Electricity and Magnetism*, 3rd ed. 2 vols. 42s.

—— *Electric Lighting*, 18s.

—— *School Electricity*, 5s.

—— Mrs. J. E. H., *Decorative Electricity*, illust. 12s.

GOWER, LORD RONALD, *Handbook to the Art Galleries of Belgium and Holland*, 5s.

—— *Northbrook Gallery*, 63s. and 105s.

—— *Portraits at Castle Howard*. 2 vols. 126s.

—— See also Great Artists.

GRAESSI, *Italian Dictionary*, 3s. 6d.; roan, 5s.

GRAY, T. See Choice Eds.

Great Artists, Biographies, illustrated, emblematical binding, 3s. 6d. per vol. except where the price is given.

Barbizon School, 2 vols.
Claude le Lorrain.
Correggio, 2s. 6d.
Cox and De Wint.
George Cruikshank.
Della Robbia and Cellini, 2s. 6d.
Albrecht Dürer.
Figure Paintings of Holland.
Fra Angelico, Masaccio, &c.
Fra Bartolommeo, &c.
Gainsborough and Constable.
Ghiberti and Donatello, 2s. 6d.
Giotto, by H. Quilter, 15s.
Hogarth, by A. Dobson.
Hans Holbein.
Landscape Painters of Holland.
Landseer.
Leonardo da Vinci.
Little Masters of Germany, by Scott; éd. de luxe, 10s. 6d.
Mantegna and Francia.
Meissonier, 2s. 6d.
Michelangelo.
Mulready.
Murillo, by Minor, 2s. 6d.
Overbeck.
Raphael.

Great Artists—continued.
Rembrandt.
Reynolds.
Romney and Lawrence, 2s. 6d.
Rubens, by Kett.
Tintoretto, by Osler.
Titian, by Heath.
Turner, by Monkhouse.
Vandyck and Hals.
Velasquez.
Vernet & Delaroche.
Watteau, by Mollett, 2s. 6d.
Wilkie, by Mollett.

Great Musicians, edited by F. Hueffer. A series of biographies, 3s. each:—
Bach, by Poole.
Beethoven.
*Berlioz.
Cherubini.
English Church Composers.
*Glück.
Handel.
Haydn.
*Marcello.
Mendelssohn.
Mozart.
*Palestrina and the Roman School.
Purcell.
Rossini and Modern Italian School.
Schubert.
Schumann.
Richard Wagner.
Weber.
    * *Are not yet published.*

Greece. See Foreign Countries.

GRIEB, *German Dictionary*, n. ed. 2 vols. 21s.

GRIMM, H., *Literature*, 8s. 6d.

GROHMANN, *Camps in the Rockies*, 12s. 6d.

GROVES, J. PERCY. See Low's Standard Books.

GUIZOT, *History of England*, illust. 3 vols. re-issue at 10s. 6d. per vol.

—— *History of France*, illust. re-issue, 8 vols. 10s. 6d. each.

—— Abridged by G. Masson, 5s.

GUYON, MADAME, *Life*, 6s.

HADLEY, J., *Roman Law*, 7s. 6d.

Half-length Portraits. See Gentle Life Series.

HALFORD, F. M., *Dry Fly-fishing*, n. ed. 25s.

—— *Floating Flies*, 15s. & 30s.

HALL, *How to Live Long*, 2s.

HALSEY, F. A., *Slide Valve Gears*, 8s. 6d.

HAMILTON. See English Philosophers.

—— E. *Fly-fishing*, 6s. and 10s. 6d.

—— *Riverside Naturalist*, 14s.

HAMILTON'S *Mexican Handbook*, 8s. 6d.

HANDEL. See Great Musicians.

HANDS, T., *Numerical Exercises in Chemistry*, 2s. 6d.; without ans. 2s.; ans. sep. 6d.

Handy Guide to Dry-fly Fishing, by Cotswold Isys, 1s.

Handy Guide Book to Japanese Islands, 6s. 6d.

HARDY, A. S., *Passe-rose*, 6s.

—— THOS. See Low's Standard Novels.

HARKUT, F., *Conspirator*, 6s.

HARLAND, MARION, *Home Kitchen*, 5s.

Harper's Young People, vols. I.—VII. 7s. 6d. each; gilt 8s.

HARRIES, A. See Nursing Record Series.

HARRIS, W. B., *Land of the African Sultan*, 10s. 6d.; l. p. 31s. 6d.

HARRISON, MARY, *Modern Cookery*, 6s.

—— *Skilful Cook*, n. ed. 5s.

—— MRS. B. *Old-fashioned Fairy Book*, 6s.

—— W., *London Houses*, Illust. n. edit. 1s. 6d., 6s. nett; & 2s. 6d.

HARTLEY and MILL. See English Philosophers.
HATTON, Joseph, *Journalistic London*, 12s. 6d.
—— See also Low's Standard Novels.
HAWEIS, H.R., *Broad Church*, 6s.
—— *Poets in the Pulpit*, 10s. 6d. new edit. 6s.; also 3s. 6d.
—— Mrs., *Housekeeping*, 2s. 6d.
—— *Beautiful Houses*, 4s., new edit. 1s.
HAYDN. See Great Musicians.
HAZLITT, W., *Round Table*, 2s 6d.
HEAD, Percy R. See Illus. Text Books and Great Artists.
HEARD, A.F., *Russian Church*, 16s.
HEARN, L., *Youma*, 5s.
HEATH, F. G., *Fern World*, 12s. 6d., new edit. 6s.
—— Gertrude, *Tell us Why*, 2s. 6d.
HELDMANN, B., *Mutiny of the "Leander,"* 7s. 6d. and 5s.
—— See also Low's Standard Books for Boys.
HENTY, G. A., *Hidden Foe*, 2 vols. 21s.
—— See also Low's Standard Books for Boys.
—— Richmond, *Australiana*, 5s.
HERBERT, T., *Salads and Sandwiches*, 6d.
HICKS, C. S., *Our Boys, and what to do with Them; Merchant Service*, 5s.
—— *Yachts, Boats, and Canoes*, 10s. 6d.
HIGGINSON, T. W., *Atlantic Essays*, 6s.
—— *History of the U.S.*, illust. 14s.

HILL, A. Staveley, *From Home to Home in N.-W. Canada*, 21s., new edit. 7s. 6d.
—— G. B., *Footsteps of Johnson*, 63s,; édition de luxe, 147s.
HINMAN, R., *Eclectic Physical Geography*, 5s.
Hints on proving Wills without Professional Assistance, n. ed. 1s.
HOEY, Mrs. Cashel. See Low's Standard Novels.
HOFFER, *Caoutchouc & Gutta Percha*, 12s. 6d.
HOGARTH. See Gr. Artists.
HOLBEIN. See Great Artists.
HOLDER, Charles F., *Ivory King*, 8s. 6d.
—— *Living Lights*, 8s. 6d.
—— *Marvels of Animal Life*, 8s. 6d.
HOLM, Saxe, *Draxy Miller*, 2s. 6d. and 2s.
HOLMES, O. Wendell, *Before the Curfew*, 5s.
—— *Over the Tea Cups*, 6s.
—— *Iron Gate, &c., Poems*, 6s.
—— *Last Leaf*, 42s.
—— *Mechanism in Thought and Morals*, 1s. 6d.
—— *Mortal Antipathy*, 8s. 6d., 2s. and 1s.
—— *Our Hundred Days in Europe*, new edit. 6s.; l. paper 15s.
—— *Poetical Works*, new edit., 2 vols. 10s. 6d.
—— *Works*, prose, 10 vols.; poetry, 4 vols.; 14 vols. 84s. Limited large paper edit., 14 vols. 294s. nett.
—— See also Low's Standard Novels and Rose Library.
HOLUB, E., *South Africa*, 2 vols. 42s.
HOPKINS, Manley, *Treatise on the Cardinal Numbers*, 2s. 6d.

Horace in Latin, with Smart's literal translation, 2s. 6d.; translation only, 1s. 6d.
HORETZKY, C., *Canada on the Pacific*, 5s.
How and where to Fish in Ireland, by H. Regan, 3s. 6d.
HOWARD, BLANCHE W., *Tony the Maid*, 3s. 6d.
—— See also Low's Standard Novels.
HOWELLS, W. D., *Suburban Sketches*, 7s. 6d.
—— *Undiscovered Country*, 3s. 6d. and 1s.
HOWORTH, H. H., *Glacial Nightmare*, 18s.
—— *Mammoth and the Flood*, 18s.
HUDSON, N. H., *Purple Land that England Lost; Banda Oriental* 2 vols. 21s.: 1 vol. 6s.
HUEFFER, E. See Great Musicians.
HUGHES, HUGH PRICE. See Preachers.
HUME, F., *Creature of the Night*, 1s.
Humorous Art at the Naval Exhibition, 1s.
HUMPHREYS, JENNET, *Some Little Britons in Brittany*, 2s. 6d.
Hundred Greatest Men, new edit. one vol. 21s.
HUNTINGDON, *The Squire's Nieces*, 2s. 6d. (Playtime Library.)
HYDE, *Hundred Years by Post*, 1s.
Hymnal Companion to the Book of Common Prayer, separate lists gratis.
Iceland. See Foreign Countries.
Illustrated Text-Books of Art-Education, edit. by E. J. Poynter, R.A., illust. 5s. each.
Architecture, Classic and Early Christian.

Illust. Text-Books—continued.
Architecture, Gothic and Renaissance.
German, Flemish, and Dutch Painting.
Painting, Classic and Italian.
Painting, English and American.
Sculpture, modern.
Sculpture, by G. Redford.
Spanish and French artists.
INDERWICK, F. A., *Interregnum*, 10s. 6d.
—— *Sidelights on the Stuarts*, new edit. 7s. 6d.
INGELOW, JEAN. See Low's Standard Novels.
INGLIS, *Our New Zealand Cousins*, 6s.
—— *Sport and Work on the Nepaul Frontier*, 21s.
—— *Tent Life in Tiger Land*, 18s.
IRVING, W., *Little Britain*, 10s. 6d. and 6s.
—— Works, "Geoffrey Crayon" edit. 27 vols. 16l. 16s.
JACKSON, J., *Handwriting in Relation to Hygiene*, 3d.
—— *New Style Vertical Writing Copy-Books*, Series I. 1—8, 2d. and 1d. each.
—— *New Code Copy-Books*, 22 Nos. 2d. each.
—— *Shorthand of Arithmetic, Companion to all Arithmetics*, 1s. 6d.
—— L., *Ten Centuries of European Progress*, with maps, 12s. 6d.
JAMES, CROAKE, *Law and Lawyers*, new edit. 7s. 6d.
—— HENRY. See Daudet, A.
JAMES and MOLÉ'S *French Dictionary*, 3s. 6d. cloth; roan, 5s.
JAMES, *German Dictionary*, 3s. 6d. cloth; roan 5s.
JANVIER, *Aztec Treasure House*, 7s. 6d.; new edit. 5s.

Japan. See Foreign Countries.
JEFFERIES, RICHARD, *Amaryllis at the Fair*, 7s. 6d.
—— *Bevis*, new edit. 5s.
JEPHSON, A. J. M., *Emin Pasha relief expedition*, 21s.
JERDON. See Low's Standard Series.
JOHNSTON, H. H., *The Congo*, 21s.
JOHNSTON-LAVIS, H. J., *South Italian Volcanoes*, 15s.
JOHNSTONE, D. L., *Land of the Mountain Kingdom*, new edit. 3s. 6d. and 2s. 6d.
JONES, MRS. HERBERT, *Sandringham, Past and Present*, illust., new edit. 8s. 6d.
JULIEN, F., *Conversational French Reader*, 2s. 6d.
—— *English Student's French Examiner*, 2s.
—— *First Lessons in Conversational French Grammar*, n. ed. 1s.
—— *French at Home and at School*, Book I. accidence, 2s.; key, 3s.
—— *Petites Leçons de Conversation et de Grammaire*, n. ed. 3s.
—— *Petites Leçons*, with phrases, 3s. 6d.
—— *Phrases of Daily Use*, separately, 6d.
KARR, H. W. SETON, *Shores and Alps of Alaska*, 16s.
KARSLAND, VEVA, *Women and their Work*, 1s.
KAY. See Foreign Countries.
KENNEDY, E. B., *Blacks and Bushrangers*, new edit. 5s., 3s. 6d. and 2s. 6d.
KERR, W. M., *Far Interior, the Cape, Zambesi, &c.*, 2 vols. 32s.
KERSHAW, S. W., *Protestants from France in their English Home*, 6s.
KETT, C. W., *Rubens*, 3s. 6d.

Khedives and Pashas, 7s. 6d.
KILNER, E. A., *Four Welsh Counties*, 5s.
King and Commons. See Cavalier in Bayard Series.
KINGSLEY, R. G., *Children of Westminster Abbey*, 5s.
KINGSTON. See Low's Standard Books.
KIPLING, RUDYARD, *Soldiers Three, &c.*, stories, 1s.
—— *Story of the Gadsbys*, new edit. 1s.
—— *In Black and White, &c.*, stories, 1s.
—— *Wee Willie Winkie, &c.*, stories, 1s.
—— *Under the Deodars, &c.*, stories, 1s.
—— *Phantom Rickshaw, &c.*, stories, 1s.
*** The six collections of stories may also be had in 2 vols. 3s. 6d. each.
—— *Stories*, Library Edition, 2 vols. 6s. each.
KIRKALDY, W. G., *David Kirkaldy's Mechanical Testing*, 84s.
KNIGHT, A. L., *In the Web of Destiny*, 7s. 6d.
—— E. F., *Cruise of the Falcon*, new edit. 3s. 6d.
—— E. J., *Albania and Montenegro*, 12s. 6d.
—— V. C., *Church Unity*, 5s.
KNOX, T. W., *Boy Travellers*, new edit. 5s.
KNOX-LITTLE, W. J., *Sermons*, 3s. 6d.
KUNHARDT, C. P., *Small Yachts*, new edit. 50s.
—— *Steam Yachts*, 16s.
KWONG, *English Phrases*, 21s.
LABOULAYE, E., *Abdallah*, 2s. 6d.
LALANNE, *Etching*, 12s. 6d.

LAMB, CHAS., *Essays of Elia*, with designs by C. O. Murray, 6s.
LAMBERT, *Angling Literature*, 3s. 6d.
Landscape Painters of Holland. See Great Artists.
LANDSEER. See Great Artists.
LANGLEY, S. P., *New Astronomy*, 10s. 6d.
LANIER, S., *Boy's Froissart*, 7s. 6d.; *King Arthur*, 7s. 6d.; *Mabinogion*, 7s. 6d.; *Percy*, 7s. 6d.
LANSDELL, HENRY, *Through Siberia*, 1 v. 15s. and 10s. 6d.
—— *Russia in Central Asia*, 2 vols. 42s.
—— *Through Central Asia*, 12s.
LARDEN, W., *School Course on Heat*, n. ed. 5s.
LAURIE, A., *Secret of the Magian, the Mystery of Ecbatana*, illus. 6s. See also Low's Standard Books.
LAWRENCE, SERGEANT, *Autobiography*, 6s.
—— and ROMNEY. See Great Artists.
LAYARD, MRS., *West Indies*, 2s. 6d.
LEA, H. C., *Inquisition*, 3 vols. 42s.
LEARED, A., *Marocco*, n. ed. 16s.
LEAVITT, *New World Tragedies*, 7s. 6d.
LEFFINGWELL, W. B., *Shooting*, 18s.
—— *Wild Fowl Shooting*, 10s. 6d.
LEFROY, W., DEAN. See Preachers.
LELAND, C. G., *Algonquin Legends*, 8s.
LEMON, M., *Small House over the Water*, 6s.

Leo XIII. Life, 18s.
Leonardo da Vinci. See Great Artists.
—— *Literary Works*, by J. P. Richter, 2 vols. 252s.
LIEBER, *Telegraphic Cipher*, 42s. nett.
Like unto Christ. See Gentle Life Series.
LITTLE, ARCH. J., *Yang-tse Gorges*, n. ed., 10s. 6d.
Little Masters of Germany. See Great Artists.
LONGFELLOW, *Miles Standish*, illus. 21s.
—— *Maidenhood*, with col. pl. 2s. 6d.; gilt edges, 3s. 6d.
—— *Nuremberg*, photogr. illu. 31s. 6d.
—— *Song of Hiawatha*, illust. 21s.
LOOMIS, E., *Astronomy*, n. ed. 8s. 6d.
LORNE, MARQUIS OF, *Canada and Scotland*, 7s. 6d.
—— *Palmerston.* See Prime Ministers.
Louis, St. See Bayard Series.
Low's French Readers, edit. by C. F. Clifton, I. 3d., II. 3d., III. 6d.
—— *German Series.* See Goethe, Meissner, Sandars, and Schiller.
—— *London Charities*, annually, 1s. 6d.; sewed, 1s.
—— *Illustrated Germ. Primer*, 1s.
—— *Infant Primers*, I. illus. 3d.; II. illus. 6d. and 7d.
—— *Pocket Encyclopædia*, with plates, 3s. 6d.; roan, 4s. 6d.
—— *Readers*, I., 9d.; II., 10d.; III., 1s.; IV., 1s. 3d.; V., 1s. 4d.; VI., 1s. 6d.

Low's Select Parchment Series.
Aldrich (T. B.) Friar Jerome's Beautiful Book, 3s. 6d.
Lewis (Rev. Gerrard), Ballads of the Cid, 2s. 6d.
Whittier (J. G.) The King's Missive. 3s. 6d.

Low's Stand. Library of Travel (except where price is stated), per volume, 7s. 6d.
1. Butler, Great Lone Land; also 3s. 6d.
2. —— Wild North Land.
3. Stanley (H. M.) Coomassie, 3s. 6d.
4. —— How I Found Livingstone; also 3s. 6d.
5. —— Through the Dark Continent, 1 vol. illust., 12s. 6d.; also 3s. 6d.
8. MacGahan (J. A.) Oxus.
9. Spry, voyage, *Challenger*.
10. Burnaby's Asia Minor, 10s. 6d.
11. Schweinfurth's Heart of Africa, 2 vols. 15s.; also 3s. 6d. each.
12. Marshall (W.) Through America.
13. Lansdell (H.) Through Siberia, 10s. 6d.
14. Coote, South by East, 10s. 6d.
15. Knight, Cruise of the *Falcon*, also 3s. 6d.
16. Thomson (Joseph) Through Masai Land.
19. Ashe (R. P.) Two Kings of Uganda, 3s. 6d.

Low's Standard Novels (except where price is stated), 6s.
Baker, John Westacott.
Black (W.) Craig Royston.
—— Daughter of Heth.
—— House Boat.
—— In Far Lochaber.
—— In Silk Attire.
—— Kilmeny.
—— Lady Siverdale's Sweetheart.
—— New Prince Fortunatus.
—— Penance of John Logan.
—— Stand Fast, Craig Royston!
—— Sunrise.
—— Three Feathers.

Low's Stand. Novels—continued.
Blackmore (R. D.) Alice Lorraine.
—— Christowell.
—— Clara Vaughan.
—— Cradock Nowell.
—— Cripps the Carrier.
—— Eremo, or My Father's Sins.
—— Kit and Kitty.
—— Lorna Doone.
—— Mary Anerley.
—— Sir Thomas Upmore.
—— Springhaven.
Brémont, Gentleman Digger.
Brown (Robert) Jack Abbott's Log.
Bynner, Agnes Surriage.
—— Begum's Daughter.
Cable (G. W.) Bonaventure, 5s.
Coleridge (C. R.) English Squire.
Craddock, Despot of Broomsedge.
Croker (Mrs. B. M.) Some One Else.
Cumberland (Stuart) Vasty Deep.
De Leon, Under the Stars and Crescent.
Edwards (Miss Betham) Half-way.
Eggleston, Juggernaut.
French Heiress in her own Chateau.
Gilliat (E.) Story of the Dragonnades.
Hardy (A. S.) Passe-rose.
—— (Thos.) Far from the Madding.
—— Hand of Ethelberta.
—— Laodicean.
—— Mayor of Casterbridge.
—— Pair of Blue Eyes.
—— Return of the Native.
—— Trumpet-Major.
—— Two on a Tower.
Harkut, Conspirator.
Hatton (J.) Old House at Sandwich.
—— Three Recruits.
Hoey (Mrs. Cashel) Golden Sorrow.
—— Out of Court.
—— Stern Chase.
Howard (Blanche W.) Open Door.
Ingelow (Jean) Don John.
—— John Jerome, 5s.
—— Sarah de Berenger.
Lathrop, Newport, 6s.
Mac Donald (Geo.) Adela Cathcart.
—— Guild Court.

Low's Stand. Novels—continued.
Mac Donald (Geo.) Mary Marston.
—— Orts.
—— Stephen Archer, &c.
—— The Vicar's Daughter.
—— Weighed and Wanting.
Macmaster, Our Pleasant Vices.
Macquoid (Mrs.) Diane.
Musgrave (Mrs.) Miriam.
Osborn, Spell of Ashtaroth, 5s.
Prince Maskiloff.
Riddell (Mrs.) Alaric Spenceley.
—— Daisies and Buttercups.
—— Senior Partner.
—— Struggle for Fame.
Russell (W. Clark) Betwixt the Forelands.
—— Frozen Pirate.
—— Jack's Courtship.
—— John Holdsworth.
—— Little Loo.
—— My Watch Below.
—— Ocean Free Lance.
—— Sailor's Sweetheart.
—— Sea Queen.
—— Strange Voyage.
—— The Lady Maud.
—— Wreck of the *Grosvenor*.
Stenart, Kilgroom.
Stockton (F. R.) Ardis Claverden.
—— Bee-man of Orn, 5s.
—— Hundredth Man.
—— The late Mrs. Null.
Stoker, Snake's Pass.
Stowe (Mrs.) Old Town Folk.
—— Poganuc People.
Thomas, House on the Scar.
Thomson, Ula, an African Romance.
Tourgee, Murvale Eastman.
Tytler (S.) Duchess Frances.
Vane, From the Dead.
Wallace (Lew.) Ben Hur.
Warner, Little Journey in the World.
Woolson (Constance Fenimore) Anne.
—— East Angles.
—— For the Major, 5s.
—— Jupiter Lights.
See also Sea Stories.

Low's Stand. Novels, new issue at short intervals, 2s. 6d. and 2s.
Blackmore, Alice Lorraine.
—— Christowell.
—— Clara Vaughan.
—— Cripps the Carrier.
—— Kit and Kitty.
—— Lorna Doone.
—— Mary Anerley.
—— Tommy Upmore.
Cable, Bonaventure.
Croker, Some One Else.
Cumberland, Vasty Deep.
De Leon, Under the Stars.
Edwards, Half-way.
Hardy, Laodicean.
—— Madding Crowd.
—— Mayor of Casterbridge.
—— Trumpet-Major.
—— Two on a Tower.
Hatton, Old House at Sandwich.
—— Three Recruits.
Hoey, Golden Sorrow.
—— Out of Court.
—— Stern Chase.
Holmes, Guardian Angel.
Ingelow, John Jerome.
—— Sarah de Berenger.
Mac Donald, Adela Cathcart.
—— Guild Court.
—— Stephen Archer.
—— Vicar's Daughter.
Oliphant, Innocent.
Riddell, Daisies and Buttercups.
—— Senior Partner.
Stockton, Bee-man of Orn, 5s.
—— Dusantes.
—— Mrs. Leeks and Mrs. Aleshine.
Stowe, Dred.
—— Old Town Folk.
—— Poganuc People.'
Thomson, Ula.
Walford, Her Great Idea, &c., Stories.
Low's German Series, a graduated course. See "German."
Low's Readers. See English Reader and French Reader.
Low's Standard Books for Boys, with numerous illustrations, 2s. 6d. each; gilt edges, 3s. 6d.

Low's Stand. Books for Boys—
continued.

Adventures in New Guinea: the Narrative of Louis Tregance.
Biart (Lucien) Adventures of a Young Naturalist.
—— My Rambles in the New World.
Boussenard, Crusoes of Guiana.
—— Gold Seekers, a sequel to the above.
Butler (Col. Sir Wm., K.C.B.) Red Cloud, the Solitary Sioux: a Tale of the Great Prairie.
Cahun (Leon) Adventures of Captain Mago.
—— Blue Banner.
Célière, Startling Exploits of the Doctor.
Chaillu (Paul du) Wild Life under the Equator.
Collingwood (Harry) Under the Meteor Flag.
—— Voyage of the *Aurora*.
Cozzens (S. W.) Marvellous Country.
Dodge (Mrs.) Hans Brinker; or, The Silver Skates.
Du Chaillu (Paul) Stories of the Gorilla Country.
Erckmann-Chatrian, Brothers Rantzau.
Fenn (G. Manville) Off to the Wilds.
—— Silver Cañon.
Groves (Percy) Charmouth Grange; a Tale of the 17th Century.
Heldmann (B.) Mutiny on Board the Ship *Leander*.
Henty (G. A.) Cornet of Horse: a Tale of Marlborough's Wars.
—— Jack Archer; a Tale of the Crimea.
—— Winning his Spurs: a Tale of the Crusades.
Johnstone (D. Lawson) Mountain Kingdom.
Kennedy (E. B.) Blacks and Bushrangers in Queensland.
Kingston (W. H. G.) Ben Burton; or, Born and Bred at Sea.
—— Captain Mugford; or, Our Salt and Fresh Water Tutors.
—— Dick Cheveley.
—— Heir of Kilfinnan.

Low's Stand. Books for Boys—
continued.

Kingston (W. H. G.) Snowshoes and Canoes.
—— Two Supercargoes.
—— With Axe and Rifle on the Western Prairies.
Laurie (A.) Conquest of the Moon.
—— New York to Brest in Seven Hours.
MacGregor (John) A Thousand Miles in the *Rob Roy* Canoe on Rivers and Lakes of Europe.
Maclean (H. E.) Maid of the Ship *Golden Age*.
Meunier, Great Hunting Grounds of the World.
Muller, Noble Words and Deeds.
Perelaer, The Three Deserters; or, Ran Away from the Dutch.
Reed (Talbot Baines) Sir Ludar: a Tale of the Days of the Good Queen Bess.
Rousselet (Louis) Drummer-boy: a Story of the Time of Washington.
—— King of the Tigers.
—— Serpent Charmer.
—— Son of the Constable of France.
Russell (W. Clark) Frozen Pirates.
Stanley, My Kalulu—Prince, King and Slave.
Winder (F. H.) Lost in Africa.

Low's Standard Series of Books by popular writers, cloth gilt, 2s.; gilt edges, 2s. 6d. each.

Alcott (L. M.) A Rose in Bloom.
—— An Old-Fashioned Girl.
—— Aunt Jo's Scrap Bag.
—— Eight Cousins, illust.
—— Jack and Jill.
—— Jimmy's Cruise.
—— Little Men.
—— Little Women and Little Women Wedded.
—— Lulu's Library, illust.
—— Shawl Straps.
—— Silver Pitchers.
—— Spinning-Wheel Stories.
—— Under the Lilacs, illust.
—— Work and Beginning Again, ill.

Low's Stand. Series—continued.
Alden (W. L.) Jimmy Brown, illust.
—— Trying to Find Europe.
Bunyan (John) Pilgrim's Progress, (extra volume), gilt, 2s.
De Witt (Madame) An Only Sister.
Francis (Francis) Eric and Ethel, illust.
Holm (Saxe) Draxy Miller's Dowry.
Jerdon (Gert.) Keyhole Country, illust.
Robinson (Phil) In My Indian Garden.
—— Under the Punkah.
Roe (E. P.) Nature's Serial Story.
Saintine, Picciola.
Samuels, Forecastle to Cabin, illust.
Sandeau (Jules) Seagull Rock.
Stowe (Mrs.) Dred.
—— Ghost in the Mill, &c.
—— My Wife and I.
—— We and our Neighbours.
See also Low's Standard Series.
Tooley (Mrs.) Life of Harriet Beecher Stowe.
Warner (C. Dudley) In the Wilderness.
—— My Summer in a Garden.
Whitney (Mrs.) A Summer in Leslie Goldthwaite's Life.
—— Faith Gartney's Girlhood.
—— Hitherto.
—— Real Folks.
—— The Gayworthys.
—— We Girls.
—— The Other Girls: a Sequel.
⁎⁎* A new illustrated list of books for boys and girls, with portraits of celebrated authors, sent post free on application.*

LOWELL, J. R., *Among my Books*, Series I. and II., 7s. 6d. each.
—— *My Study Windows*, n. ed. 1s.
—— *Vision of Sir Launfal*, illus. 63s.
MACDONALD, A., *Our Sceptred Isle*, 3s. 6d.
—— D., *Oceania*, 6s.

MACDONALD, GEO., *Castle Warlock, a Homely Romance*, 3 vols. 31s. 6d.
—— See also Low's Standard Novels.
—— SIR JOHN A., *Life*.
MACDOWALL, ALEX. B., *Curve Pictures of London*, 1s.
MACGAHAN, J. A., *Oxus*, 7s. 6d.
MACGOUN, *Commercial Correspondence*, 5s.
MACGREGOR, J., *Rob Roy in the Baltic*, n. ed. 3s. 6d. and 2s. 6d.
—— *Rob Roy Canoe*, new edit., 3s. 6d. and 2s. 6d.
—— *Yawl Rob Roy*, new edit., 3s. 6d. and 2s. 6d.
MACKENNA, *Brave Men in Action*. 10s. 6d.
MACKENZIE, SIR MORELL, *Fatal Illness of Frederick the Noble*, 2s. 6d.
MACKINNON and SHADBOLT, *South African Campaign*, 50s.
MACLAREN, A. See Preachers.
MACLEAN, H. E. See Low's Standard Books.
MACMASTER. See Low's Standard Novels.
MACMURDO, E., *History of Portugal*, 21s.; II. 21s.; III. 21s.
MAHAN, A. T., *Influence of Sea Power on History*, 18s.
Maid of Florence, 10s. 6d.
MAIN, Mrs., *High Life*, 10s. 6d.
—— See also Burnaby, Mrs.
MALAN, A. N., *Cobbler of Cornikeranium*, 5s.
—— C. F. DE M., *Eric and Connie's Cruise*, 5s.
Man's Thoughts. See Gentle Life Series.
MANLEY, J. J., *Fish and Fishing*, 6s.

MANTEGNA and FRANCIA. See Great Artists.

MARCH, F. A., *Comparative Anglo-Saxon Grammar*, 12s.

—— *Anglo-Saxon Reader*, 7s. 6d.

MARKHAM, ADM., *Naval Career*, 14s.

—— *Whaling Cruise*, new edit. 7s. 6d.

—— C. R., *Peru*. See Foreign Countries.

—— *Fighting Veres*, 18s.

—— *War Between Peru and Chili*, 10s. 6d.

MARSH, G. P., *Lectures on the English Language*, 18s.

—— *Origin and History of the English Language*, 18s.

MARSHALL, W. G., *Through America*, new edit. 7s. 6d.

MARSTON, E., *How Stanley wrote "In Darkest Africa,"* 1s.

—— See also Amateur Angler, Frank's Ranche, and Fresh Woods.

—— W., *Eminent Actors*, n. ed. 6s.

MARTIN, J. W., *Float Fishing and Spinning*, new edit. 2s.

Massage. See Nursing Record Series.

MATTHEWS, J. W., *Incwadi Yami*, 14s.

MAURY, M. F., *Life*, 12s. 6d.

—— *Physical Geography and Meteorology of the Sea*, new ed. 6s.

MEISSNER, A. L., *Children's Own German Book* (Low's Series), 1s. 6d.

—— *First German Reader* (Low's Series), 1s. 6d.

—— *Second German Reader* (Low's Series), 1s. 6d.

MEISSONIER. See Great Artists.

MELBOURNE, LORD. See Prime Ministers.

MELIO, G. L., *Swedish Drill*, 1s. 6d.

MENDELSSOHN *Family, 1729-1847, Letters and Journals*, 2 vols. 30s.; new edit. 30s.

—— See also Great Musicians.

MERRIFIELD, J., *Nautical Astronomy*, 7s. 6d.

MERRYLEES, J., *Carlsbad*, 7s. 6d. and 9s.

MESNEY, W., *Tungking*, 3s. 6d.

Metal Workers' Recipes and Processes, by W. T. Brannt, 12s. 6d.

MEUNIER, V. See Low's Standard Books.

Michelangelo. See Great Artists.

MILFORD, P. *Ned Stafford's Experiences*, 5s.

MILL, JAMES. See English Philosophers.

MILLS, J., *Alternative Elementary Chemistry*, 1s. 6d.

—— *Chemistry Based on the Science and Art Syllabus*, 2s. 6d.

—— *Elementary Chemistry*, answers, 2 vols. 1s. each.

MILTON'S *Allegro*. See Choice Editions.

MITCHELL, D. G. (Ik. Marvel) *English Lands, Letters and Kings*, 2 vols. 6s. each.

—— *Writings*, new edit. per vol. 5s.

MITFORD, J., *Letters*, 3s. 6d.

—— MISS, *Our Village*, illust. 5s.

Modern Etchings, 63s. & 31s. 6d.

MOLLETT, J. W., *Dictionary of Words in Art and Archæology*, illust. 15s.

—— *Etched Examples*, 31s. 6d. and 63s.

—— See also Great Artists.

MONCK. See English Philosophers.
MONEY, E., *The Truth About America*, 5s.; new edit. 2s. 6d.
MONKHOUSE. See G. Artists.
Montaigne's Essays, revised by J. Hain Friswell, 2s. 6d.
—— See Gentle Life Series.
MOORE, J. M., *New Zealand for Emigrant, Invalid, and Tourist*, 5s.
MORFILL, W. R., *Russia*, 3s. 6d.
MORLEY, HENRY, *English Literature in the Reign of Victoria*, 2s. 6d.
—— *Five Centuries of English Literature*, 2s.
MORSE, E. S., *Japanese Homes*, new edit. 10s. 6d.
MORTEN, *Hospital Life*, 1s.
MORTIMER, J., *Chess Player's Pocket-Book*, new edit. 1s.
MORWOOD, V.S., *Our Gipsies*, 18s.
MOSS, F. J., *Great South Sea*, 8s. 6d.
MOSSMAN, S., *Japan*, 3s. 6d.
MOTTI, PIETRO, *Elementary Russian Grammar*, 2s. 6d.
—— *Russian Conversation Grammar*, 5s.; Key, 2s.
MOULE, H. C. G., *Sermons*, 3s. 6d.
MOXLEY, *West India Sanatoria, and Barbados*, 3s. 6d.
MOXON, W., *Pilocereus Senilis*, 3s. 6d.
MOZART, 3s. Gr. Musicians.
MULLER, E. See Low's Standard Books.
MULLIN, J. P., *Moulding and Pattern Making*, 12s. 6d.
MULREADY, 3s. 6d. Great Artists.
MURILLO. See Great Artists.

MUSGRAVE, MRS. See Low's Standard Novels.
—— *Savage London*, n. e. 3s. 6d.
My Comforter, &c., Religious Poems, 2s. 6d.
Napoleon I. See Bayard Series.
Napoleon I. and Marie Louise, 7s. 6d.
NELSON, WOLFRED, *Panama*, 6s.
Nelson's Words and Deeds, 3s. 6d.
NETHERCOTE, *Pytchley Hunt*, 8s. 6d.
New Democracy, 1s.
New Zealand, chromos, by Barraud, 168s.
NICHOLSON, *British Association Work and Workers*, 1s.
Nineteenth Century, a Monthly Review, 2s. 6d. per No.
NISBET, HUME, *Life and Nature Studies*, 6s.
NIXON, *Story of the Transvaal*, 12s. 6d.
Nordenskiöld's Voyage, trans. 21s.
NORDHOFF, C., *California*, new edit. 12s. 6d.
NORRIS, RACHEL, *Nursing Notes*, 2s.
NORTH, W., *Roman Fever*, 25s.
Northern Fairy Tales, 5s.
NORTON, C. L., *Florida*, 5s.
NORWAY, G., *How Martin Drake Found his Father* illus. 5s.
NUGENT'S *French Dictionary*, new edit. 3s.
Nuggets of the Gough, 3s.
Nursing Record Series, text books and manuals. Edited by Charles F. Rideal.
1. Lectures to Nurses on Antiseptics in Surgery. By E. Stanmore Bishop. With coloured plates, 2s.

In all Departments of Literature.

Nursing Record Series—contin.
2. Nursing Notes. Medical and Surgical information. For Hospital Nurses, &c. With illustrations and a glossary of terms. By Rachel Norris (née Williams), late Acting Superintendent of Royal Victoria Military Hospital at Suez, 2s.
3. Practical Electro-Therapeutics. By Arthur Harries, M.D., and H. Newman Lawrence. With photographs and diagrams, 1s. 6d.
4. Massage for Beginners. Simple and easy directions for learning and remembering the different movements. By Lucy Fitch, 1s.

O'BRIEN, *Fifty Years of Concession to Ireland*, vol. i. 16s.; vol. ii. 16s.
——— *Irish Land Question*, 2s.
OGDEN, JAMES, *Fly-tying*, 2s. 6d.
O'GRADY, *Bardic Literature of Ireland*, 1s.
——— *History of Ireland*, vol. i. 7s. 6d.; ii. 7s. 6d.
Old Masters in Photo. 73s. 6d.
Orient Line Guide, new edit. 2s. 6d.
ORLEBAR, *Sancta Christina*, 5s.
Other People's Windows. See Gentle Life Series.
OTTÉ, *Denmark and Iceland*, 3s. 6d. Foreign Countries.
Our Little Ones in Heaven, 5s.
Out of School at Eton, 2s. 6d.
OVERBECK. See Great Artists.
OWEN, DOUGLAS, *Marine Insurance*, 15s.
Oxford Days, by a M.A., 2s. 6d.
PALGRAVE, *Chairman's Handbook*, new edit. 2s.
——— *Oliver Cromwell*, 10s. 6d.

PALLISER, *China Collector's Companion*, 5s.
——— *History of Lace*, n. ed. 21s.
PANTON, *Homes of Taste*, 2s. 6d.
PARKE, *Emin Pasha Relief Expedition*, 21s.
PARKER, E. H., *Chinese Account of the Opium War*, 1s. 6d.
PARSONS, J., *Principles of Partnership*, 31s. 6d.
——— T. P., *Marine Insurance*, 2 vols. 63s.
PEACH, *Annals of Swainswick*, 10s. 6d.
Peel. See Prime Ministers.
PELLESCHI, G., *Gran Chaco*, 8s. 6d.
PENNELL, H. C., *Fishing Tackle*, 2s.
——— *Sporting Fish*, 15s. & 30s.
Penny Postage Jubilee, 1s.
PERRY, NORA, *Another Flock of Girls*, illus. by Birch & Copeland, 7s. 6d.
Peru, 3s. 6d. Foreign Countries.
PHELPS, E. S., *Struggle for Immortality*, 5s.
——— SAMUEL, *Life*, by W. M. Phelps and Forbes-Robertson, 12s.
PHILLIMORE, C. M., *Italian Literature*, new. edit. 3s. 6d.
PHILLIPPS, W. M., *English Elegies*, 5s.
PHILLIPS, L. P., *Dictionary of Biographical Reference*, now. edit. 25s.
——— W., *Law of Insurance*, 2 vols. 73s. 6d.
PHILPOT, H. J., *Diabetes Mellitus*, 5s.
——— *Diet Tables*, 1s. each.
Picture Gallery of British Art. I. to VI. 18s. each.
——— *Modern Art*, 3 vols. 31s. 6d. each.

PINTO, *How I Crossed Africa*, 2 vols. 42s.
Playtime Library. See Humphrey and Huntingdon.
Pleasant History of Reynard the Fox, trans. by T. Roscoe, illus. 7s. 6d.
POCOCK, R., *Gravesend Historian*, 5s.
POE, by E. C. Stedman, 3s. 6d.
—— *Raven*, ill. by G. Doré, 63s.
Poems of the Inner Life, 5s.
Poetry of Nature. See Choice Editions.
Poetry of the Anti-Jacobin, 7s. 6d. and 21s.
POOLE, *Somerset Customs and Legends*, 5s.
—— S. LANE, *Egypt*, 3s. 6d. Foreign Countries.
POPE, *Select Poetical Works*, (Bernhard Tauchnitz Collection), 2s.
PORCHER, A., *Juvenile French Plays*, 1s.
Portraits of Racehorses, 4 vols. 126s.
POSSELT, *Structure of Fibres*, 63s.
—— *Textile Design*, illust. 28s.
POYNTER. See Illustrated Text Books.
Preachers of the Age, 3s. 6d. ea.
Living Theology, by His Grace the Archbishop of Canterbury.
The Conquering Christ, by Rev. A. Maclaren.
Verbum Crucis, by the Bishop of Derry.
Ethical Christianity, by H. P. Hughes.
Sermons, by Canon W. J. Knox-Little.
Light and Peace, by H. R. Reynolds.
Faith and Duty, by A. M. Fairbairn.
Plain Words on Great Themes, by J. O. Dykes.
Sermons, by the Bishop of Ripon.

Preachers of the Age—continued.
Sermons, by Rev. C. H. Spurgeon.
Agoniæ Christi, by Dean Lefroy, of Norwich.
Sermons, by H. C. G. Moule, M.A.
Volumes will follow in quick succession by other well-known men.
Prime Ministers, a series of political biographies, edited by Stuart J. Reid, 3s. 6d. each.
1. Earl of Beaconsfield, by J. Anthony Froude.
2. Viscount Melbourne, by Henry Dunckley ("*Verax*").
3. Sir Robert Peel, by Justin McCarthy.
4. Viscount Palmerston, by the Marquis of Lorne.
5. Earl Russell, by Stuart J. Reid.
6. Right Hon. W. E. Gladstone, by G. W. E. Russell.
7. Earl of Aberdeen, by Sir Arthur Gordon.
8. Marquis of Salisbury, by H. D. Traill.
9. Earl of Derby, by George Saintsbury.
*** *An edition, limited to 250 copies, is issued on hand-made paper, medium 8vo, bound in half vellum, cloth sides, gilt top. Price for the 9 vols. 4l. 4s. nett.*
Prince Maskiloff. See Low's Standard Novels.
Prince of Nursery Playmates, new edit. 2s. 6d.
PRITT, T. N., *Country Trout Flies*, 10s. 6d.
Reynolds. See Great Artists.
Purcell. See Great Musicians.
QUILTER, H., *Giotto, Life, &c.* 15s.
RAMBAUD, *History of Russia*, new edit., 3 vols. 21s.
RAPHAEL. See Great Artists.
REDFORD, *Sculpture.* See Illustrated Text-books.
REDGRAVE, *Engl. Painters*, 10s. 6d. and 12s.

REED, Sir E. J., *Modern Ships of War*, 10s. 6d.
—— T. B., *Roger Ingleton, Minor*, 5s.
—— Sir Ludar. See Low's Standard Books.
REID, Mayne, Capt., *Stories of Strange Adventures*, illust. 5s.
—— Stuart J. See Prime Ministers.
—— T. Wemyss, *Land of the Bey*, 10s. 6d.
Remarkable Bindings in British Museum, 168s.; 94s. 6d.; 73s. 6d. and 63s.
REMBRANDT. See Great Artists.
Reminiscences of a Boyhood, 6s.
REMUSAT, *Memoirs*, Vols. I. and II. new ed. 16s. each.
—— *Select Letters*, 16s.
REYNOLDS. See Gr. Artists.
—— Henry R., *Light & Peace, &c. Sermons*, 3s. 6d.
RICHARDS, J. W., *Aluminium*, new edit. 21s.
RICHARDSON, *Choice of Books*, 3s. 6d.
RICHTER, J. P., *Italian Art*, 42s.
—— See also Great Artists.
RIDDELL. See Low's Standard Novels.
RIDEAL, *Women of the Time*, 14s.
RIFFAULT, *Colours for Painting*, 31s. 6d.
RIIS, *How the Other Half Lives*, 10s. 6d.
RIPON, Bp. of. See Preachers.
ROBERTS, Miss, *France*. See Foreign Countries.
—— W., *English Bookselling*, earlier history. 7s. 6d.
ROBIDA, A., *Toilette*, coloured, 7s. 6d.

ROBINSON, "*Romeo*" *Coates*, 7s. 6d.
—— *Noah's Ark*, n. ed. 3s. 6d.
—— *Sinners & Saints*, 10s. 6d.
—— See also Low's Standard Series.
—— *Wealth and its Sources*, 5s.
—— W. C., *Law of Patents*, 3 vols. 105s.
ROCHEFOUCAULD. See Bayard Series.
ROCKSTRO, *History of Music*, new ed. 14s.
RODRIGUES, *Panama Canal*, 5s.
ROE, E. P. See Low's Standard Series.
ROGERS, S. See Choice Editions.
ROLFE, *Pompeii*, 7s. 6d.
Romantic Stories of the Legal Profession, 7s. 6d.
ROMNEY. See Great Artists.
ROOSEVELT, Blanche R. *Home Life of Longfellow*, 7s. 6d.
ROSE, J., *Mechanical Drawing*, 16s.
—— *Practical Machinist*, new ed. 12s. 6d.
—— *Key to Engines*, 8s. 6d.
—— *Modern Steam Engine*, 31s. 6d.
—— *Steam Boilers*, 12s. 6d.
Rose Library. Popular Literature of all countries, per vol. 1s., unless the price is given.
Alcott (L. M.) Eight Cousins, 2s.; cloth, 3s. 6d.
—— Jack and Jill, 2s.; cloth, 5s.
—— Jimmy's cruise in the *Pinafore*, 2s.; cloth, 3s. 6d.
—— Little Women.
—— Little Women Wedded; Nos. 4 and 5 in 1 vol. cloth, 3s. 6d.
—— Little Men, 2s.; cloth gilt, 3s. 6d.

Rose Library—continued.
Alcott (L. M.) Old-fashioned Girls, 2s.; cloth, 3s. 6d.
—— Rose in Bloom, 2s.; cl. 3s. 6d.
—— Silver Pitchers.
—— Under the Lilacs, 2s.; cloth, 3s. 6d.
—— Work, A Story of Experience, 2 vols. in 1, cloth, 3s. 6d.
Stowe (Mrs.) Pearl of Orr's Island.
—— Minister's Wooing.
—— We and Our Neighbours, 2s.
—— My Wife and I, 2s.
Dodge (Mrs.) Hans Brinker, or, The Silver Skates, 1s.; cloth, 5s.; 3s. 6d.; 2s. 6d.
Lowell (J. R.) My Study Windows.
Holmes (Oliver Wendell) Guardian Angel, cloth, 2s.
Warner (C. D.) My Summer in a Garden, cloth, 2s.
Stowe (Mrs.) Dred, 2s.; cloth gilt, 3s. 6d.
Carleton (W.) City Ballads, 2 vols. in 1, cloth gilt, 2s. 6d.
—— Legends, 2 vols. in 1, cloth gilt, 2s. 6d.
—— Farm Ballads, 6d. and 9d.; 3 vols. in 1, cloth gilt, 3s. 6d.
—— Farm Festivals, 3 vols. in 1, cloth gilt, 3s. 6d.
—— Farm Legends, 3 vols. in 1, cloth gilt, 3s. 6d.
Clients of Dr. Bernagius, 2 vols.
Howells (W. D.) Undiscovered Country.
Clay (C. M.) Baby Rue.
—— Story of Helen Troy.
Whitney (Mrs.) Hitherto, 2 vols. cloth, 3s. 6d.
Fawcett (E.) Gentleman of Leisure.
Butler, Nothing to Wear.
ROSS, Mars, *Cantabria*, 21s.
ROSSINI, &c., See Great Musicians.
Rothschilds, by J. Reeves, 7s. 6d.
Roughing it after Gold, by Rux, new edit. 1s.
ROUSSELET. See Low's Standard Books.

ROWBOTHAM, F. J., *Prairie Land*, 5s.
Royal Naval Exhibition, a souvenir, illus. 1s.
RUBENS. See Great Artists.
RUGGLES, H. J., *Shakespeare's Method*, 7s. 6d.
RUSSELL, G.W.E., *Gladstone*. See Prime Ministers.
—— W. Clark, Mrs. *Dines' Jewels*, 2s. 6d.
—— *Nelson's Words and Deeds*, 3s. 6d.
—— *Sailor's Language*, illus. 3s. 6d.
—— See also Low's Standard Novels and Sea Stories.
—— W. Howard, *Prince of Wales' Tour*, illust. 52s. 6d. and 84s.
Russia. See Foreign Countries.
Saints and their Symbols, 3s. 6d.
SAINTSBURY, G., *Earl of Derby*. See Prime Ministers.
SAINTINE, *Picciola*, 2s. 6d. and 2s. See Low's Standard Series.
SALISBURY, Lord. See Prime Ministers.
SAMUELS. See Low's Standard Series.
SANDARS, *German Primer*, 1s.
SANDEAU, *Seagull Rock*, 2s. and 2s. 6d. Low's Standard Series.
SANDLANDS, *How to Develop Vocal Power*, 1s.
SAUER, *European Commerce*, 5s.
—— *Italian Grammar* (Key, 2s.), 5s.
—— *Spanish Dialogues*, 2s. 6d.
—— *Spanish Grammar* (Key, 2s.), 5s.
—— *Spanish Reader*, new edit. 3s. 6d.
SAUNDERS, J., *Jaspar Deane*, 10s. 6d.

SCHAACK, M. J., *Anarchy*, 16s.
SCHAUERMANN, *Ornament for technical schools*, 10s. 6d.
SCHERER, *Essays in English Literature*, by G. Saintsbury, 6s.
SCHERR, *English Literature*, history, 8s. 6d.
SCHILLER'S *Prosa*, selections by Buchheim. Low's Series 2s. 6d.
SCHUBERT. See Great Musicians.
SCHUMANN. See Great Musicians.
SCHWEINFURTH. See Low's Standard Library.
Scientific Education of Dogs, 6s.
SCOTT, LEADER, *Renaissance of Art in Italy*, 31s. 6d.
—— See also Illust. Text-books.
—— SIR GILBERT, *Autobiography*, 18s.
—— W. B. See Great Artists.
SELMA, ROBERT, *Poems*, 5s.
SERGEANT, L. See Foreign Countries.
Shadow of the Rock, 2s. 6d.
SHAFTESBURY. See English Philosophers.
SHAKESPEARE, ed. by R. G. White, 3 vols. 36s.; édit. de luxe, 63s.
—— *Annals; Life & Work*, 2s.
—— *Hamlet*, 1603, also 1604, 7s. 6d.
—— *Hamlet*, by Karl Elze, 12s. 6d.
—— *Heroines*, by living painters, 105s.; artists' proofs, 630s.
—— *Macbeth*, with etchings, 105s. and 52s. 6d.
—— *Songs and Sonnets*. See Choice Editions.
—— *Taming of the Shrew*, adapted for drawing-room, paper wrapper, 1s.

SHEPHERD, *British School of Painting*, 2nd edit. 5s.; 3rd edit. sewed, 1s.
SHERIDAN, *Rivals*, col. plates, 52s. 6d. nett; art. pr. 105s. nett.
SHIELDS, G. O., *Big Game of North America*, 21s.
—— *Cruisings in the Cascades*, 10s. 6d.
SHOCK, W. H., *Steam Boilers*, 73s. 6d.
SIDNEY. See Gentle Life Series.
Silent Hour. See Gentle Life Series.
SIMKIN, *Our Armies*, plates in imitation of water-colour (5 parts at 1s.), 6s.
SIMSON, *Ecuador and the Putumayor*, 8s. 6d.
SKOTTOWE, *Hanoverian Kings*, new edit. 3s. 6d.
SLOANE, T. O., *Home Experiments*, 6s.
SMITH, HAMILTON, and LEGROS' *French Dictionary*, 2 vols. 16s., 21s., and 22s.
SMITH, EDWARD, *Cobbett*, 2 vols. 24s.
—— G., *Assyria*, 18s.
—— *Chaldean Account of Genesis*, new edit. by Sayce, 18s.
—— GERARD. See Illustrated Text Books.
—— T. ROGER. See Illustrated Text Books.
Socrates. See Bayard Series.
SOMERSET, *Our Village Life*, 5s.
Spain. See Foreign Countries.
SPAYTH, *Draught Player*, new edit. 12s. 6d.
SPIERS, *French Dictionary*, 2 vols. 18s., half bound, 2 vols. 21s.
SPRY. See Low's Stand. Library.

SPURGEON, C. H. See Preachers.

STANLEY, H. M., *Congo*, 2 vols. 42s. and 21s.
—— *In Darkest Africa*, 2 vols., 12s.
—— *Emin's Rescue*, 1s.
—— See also Low's Standard Library and Low's Standard Books.

START, *Exercises in Mensuration*, 8d.

STEPHENS, F. G., *Celebrated Flemish and French Pictures*, with notes, 28s.
—— See also Great Artists.

STERNE. See Bayard Series.

STERRY, J. ASHBY, *Cucumber Chronicles*, 5s.

STEUART, J. A., *Letters to Living Authors*, new edit. 2s. 6d.; édit. de luxe, 10s. 6d.
—— See also Low's Standard Novels.

STEVENS, J. W., *Practical Workings of the Leather Manufacture*, illust. 18s.
—— T., *Around the World on a Bicycle*, over 100 illust. 16s.; part II. 16s.

STEWART, DUGALD, *Outlines of Moral Philosophy*, 3s. 6d.

STOCKTON, F. R., *Casting Away of Mrs. Lecks*, 1s.
—— *The Dusantes*, a sequel, 1s.
—— *Merry Chanter*, 2s. 6d.
—— *Personally Conducted*, illust. by Joseph Pennell, 7s. 6d.
—— *Rudder Grangers Abroad*, 2s. 6d.
—— *Squirrel Inn*, illust. 6s.
—— *Story of Viteau*, illust. 5s. new edit. 3s. 6d.
—— *Three Burglars*, 1s. & 2s.
—— See also Low's Standard Novels.

STORER, F. H., *Agriculture*, 2 vols., 25s.

STOWE, EDWIN. See Great Artists.
—— MRS., *Flowers and Fruit from Her Writings*, 3s. 6d.
—— *Life . . . her own Words . . . Letters and Original Composition*, 15s.
—— *Life*, told for boys and girls, by S. A. Tooley, 5s., new edit. 2s. 6d. and 2s.
—— *Little Foxes*, cheap edit. 1s.; 4s. 6d.
—— *Minister's Wooing*, 1s.
—— *Pearl of Orr's Island*, 3s. 6d. and 1s.
—— *Uncle Tom's Cabin*, with 126 new illust. 2 vols. 18s.
—— See also Low's Standard Novels and Low's Standard Series.

STRACHAN, J., *New Guinea*, 12s.

STRANAHAN, *French Painting*, 21s.

STRICKLAND, F., *Engadine*, new edit. 5s.

STUTFIELD, *El Maghreb*, ride through Morocco, 8s. 6d.

SUMNER, C., *Memoir*, new edit. 2 vols. 36s.

Sweden and Norway. See Foreign Countries.

Sylvanus Redivivus, 10s. 6d.

SZCZEPANSKI, *Technical Literature*, a directory, 2s

TAINE, H. A., *Origines*, I. Ancient Régime, French Revolution, 3 vols.; Modern Régime, vol. I. 16s.

TAYLOR, H., *English Constitution*, 18s.
—— R. L., *Analysis Tables*, 1s.
—— *Chemistry*, 1s. 6d.

Techno-Chemical Receipt Book, 10s. 6d.

In all Departments of Literature. 29

TENNYSON. See Choice Editions.
Ten Years of a Sailor's Life, 7s. 6d.
THAUSING, *Malt and Beer,* 4s.
THEAKSTON, *British Angling Flies,* 5s.
Thomas à Kempis Birthday-Book, 3s. 6d.
—— *Daily Text-Book,* 2s. 6d.
—— See also Gentle Life Series.
THOMAS, BERTHA, *House on the Scar, Tale of South Devon,* 6s.
THOMSON, JOSEPH. See Low's Standard Library and Low's Standard Novels.
—— W., *Algebra,* 5s.; without Answers, 4s. 6d.; Key, 1s. 6d.
THORNTON, W. PUGIN, *Heads, and what they tell us,* 1s.
THORODSEN, J. P., *Lad and Lass,* 6s.
TICKNOR, G., *Memoir,* new edit., 2 vols. 21s.
TILESTON, MARY W., *Daily Strength,* 4s. 6d.
TINTORETTO. See Great Artists.
TITIAN. See Great Artists.
TODD, *Life,* by J. E. Todd, 12s.
TOURGÉE. See Low's Standard Novels.
TOY, C. H., *Judaism,* 14s.
Tracks in Norway, 2s., n. ed. 1s.
TRAILL. See Prime Ministers.
Transactions of the Hong Kong Medical Society, vol. I. 12s. 6d.
TROMHOLT, *Aurora Borealis,* 2 vols., 30s.
TUCKER, *Eastern Europe,* 15s.
TUCKERMAN, B., *English Fiction,* 8s. 6d.
—— *Lafayette,* 2 vols. 12s.
TURNER, J. M. W. See Gr. Artists.

TYSON, *Arctic Adventures,* 25s.
TYTLER, SARAH. See Low's Standard Novels.
—— M. C., *American Literature,* vols. I. and II. 24s.
UPTON, H., *Dairy Farming,* 2s.
Valley Council, by P. Clarke, 6s.
VANDYCK and HALS. See Great Artists.
VANE, DENZIL, *Lynn's Court Mystery,* 1s.
—— See also Low's Standard Novels.
Vane, Young Sir Harry, 18s.
VELAZQUEZ. See Gr. Artists.
—— and MURILLO, by C. B. Curtis, with etchings, 31s. 6d. and 63s.
VERE, SIR F., *Fighting Veres,* 18s.
VERNE, J., *Works by.* See page 31.
Vernet and Delaroche. See Great Artists.
VERSCHUUR, G., *At the Antipodes,* 7s. 6d.
VIGNY, *Cinq Mars,* with etchings, 2 vols. 30s.
VINCENT, F., *Through and through the Tropics,* 10s. 6d.
—— Mrs. H., *40,000 Miles over Land and Water,* 2 vols. 21s.; also 3s. 6d.
VIOLLET-LE-DUC, *Architecture,* 2 vols. 31s. 6d. each.
WAGNER. See Gr. Musicians.
WALERY, *Our Celebrities,* vol. II. part i., 30s.
WALFORD, Mrs. L. B. See Low's Standard Novels.
WALL, *Tombs of the Kings of England,* 21s.
WALLACE, L., *Ben Hur,* 2s. 6d.
—— *Boyhood of Christ,* 15s.
—— See also Low's Stand. Novs.

WALLACE, R., *Rural Economy of Australia and New Zealand*, illust. 21s. nett.

WALLER, C. H., *Names on the Gates of Pearl*, 3s. 6d.

—— *Silver Sockets*, 6s.

WALTON, *Angler*, Lea and Dove edit. by R. B. Marston, with photos., 210s. and 105s.

—— *Wallet-book*, 21s. & 42s.

—— T. H., *Coal-mining*, 25s.

WARNER, C. D., *Their Pilgrimage*, illust. by C. S. Reinhard, 7s. 6d.

—— See also Low's Standard Novels and Low's Standard Series.

WARREN, W. F., *Paradise Found, Cradle of the Human Race*, illust. 12s. 6d.

WASHBURNE, *Recollections (Siege of Paris, &c.)*, 2 vols. 36s.

WATTEAU. See Great Artists.

WEBER. See Great Musicians.

WEBSTER, *Spain*. See Foreign Countries and British Colonies.

WELLINGTON. See Bayard Series.

WELLS, H. P., *Salmon Fisherman*, 6s.

—— *Fly-rods and Tackle*, 10s. 6d.

—— J. W., *Brazil*, 2 vols. 32s.

WENZEL, *Chemical Products of the German Empire*, 25s.

West Indies. See Foreign Countries.

WESTGARTH, *Australasian Progress*, 12s.

WESTOBY, *Postage Stamps; a descriptive Catalogue*, 6s.

WHITE, Rhoda E., *From Infancy to Womanhood*, 10s. 6d.

—— R. Grant, *England without and within*, new ed. 10s. 6d.

—— *Every-day English*, 10s. 6d.

WHITE, R. Grant, *Studies in Shakespeare*, 10s. 6d.

—— *Words and their Uses*, new edit. 5s.

—— W., *Our English Homer, Shakespeare and his Plays*, 6s.

WHITNEY, Mrs. See Low's Standard Series.

WHITTIER, *St. Gregory's Guest*, 5s.

—— *Text and Verse for Every Day in the Year*, selections, 1s. 6d.

WHYTE, *Asia to Europe*, 12s.

WIKOFF, *Four Civilizations*, 6s.

WILKES, G., *Shakespeare*, 16s.

WILKIE. See Great Artists.

WILLS, *Persia as it is*, 8s. 6d.

WILSON, *Health for the People*, 7s. 6d.

WINDER, *Lost in Africa*. See Low's Standard Books.

WINSOR, J., *Columbus*, 21s.

—— *History of America*, 8 vols. per vol. 30s. and 63s.

WITTHAUS, *Chemistry*, 16s.

WOOD, *Sweden and Norway*. See Foreign Countries.

WOLLYS, *Vegetable Kingdom*, 5s.

WOOLSEY, *Communism and Socialism*, 7s. 6d.

—— *International Law*, 6th ed. 18s.

—— *Political Science*, 2 vols. 30s.

WOOLSON, C. Fenimore. See Low's Standard Novels.

WORDSWORTH. See Choice Editions.

Wreck of the "Grosvenor," 6d.

WRIGHT, H., *Friendship of God*, 6s.

—— T., *Town of Cowper*, 6s.

WRIGLEY, *Algiers Illust.* 45s

Written to Order, 6s.

BOOKS BY JULES VERNE.

WORKS. (Large Crown 8vo.)	Containing 350 to 600 pp. and from 50 to 100 full-page illustrations.		Containing the whole of text with some illustrations	
	Handsome cloth binding, gilt edges.	Plainer binding, plain edges.	Cloth binding, gilt edges, smaller type.	Limp cloth
	s. d.	s. d.	s. d.	s. d.
20,000 Leagues under the Sea. Parts I. and II.	10 6	5 0	3 6	2 0
Hector Servadac	10 6	5 0	3 6	2 0
The Fur Country	10 6	5 0	3 6	2 0
The Earth to the Moon and a Trip round it	10 6	5 0	2 vols., 2s. ea.	2 vols., 1s. ea.
Michael Strogoff	10 6	5 0	3 6	2 0
Dick Sands, the Boy Captain	10 6	5 0	3 6	2 0
Five Weeks in a Balloon	7 6	3 6	2 0	1 0
Adventures of Three Englishmen and Three Russians	7 6	3 6	2 0	1 0
Round the World in Eighty Days	7 6	3 6	2 0	1 0
A Floating City	7 6	3 6	2 0	1 0
The Blockade Runners			2 0	1 0
Dr. Ox's Experiment	—	—	2 0	1 0
A Winter amid the Ice	—	—	2 0	1 0
Survivors of the "Chancellor"	7 6	3 6	3 6	2 0
Martin Paz			2 0	1 0
The Mysterious Island, 3 vols.:—	23 6	10 6	6 0	3 0
I. Dropped from the Clouds	7 6	3 6	2 0	1 0
II. Abandoned	7 6	3 6	2 0	1 0
III. Secret of the Island	7 6	3 6	2 0	1 0
The Child of the Cavern	7 6	3 6	2 0	1 0
The Begum's Fortune	7 6	3 6	2 0	1 0
The Tribulations of a Chinaman	7 6	3 6	2 0	1 0
The Steam House, 2 vols.:—				
I. Demon of Cawnpore	7 6	3 6	2 0	1 0
II. Tigers and Traitors	7 6	3 6	2 0	1 0
The Giant Raft, 2 vols.:—				
I. 800 Leagues on the Amazon	7 6	3 6	2 0	1 0
II. The Cryptogram	7 6	3 6	2 0	1 0
The Green Ray	5 0	3 6	2 0	1 0
Godfrey Morgan	7 6	3 6	2 0	1 0
Kéraban the Inflexible:—				
I. Captain of the "Guidara"	7 6	3 6	2 0	1 0
II. Scarpante the Spy	7 6	3 6	2 0	1 0
The Archipelago on Fire	7 6	3 6	2 0	1 0
The Vanished Diamond	7 6	3 6	2 0	1 0
Mathias Sandorf	10 6	5 0	3 6	2 vols. 0 0 ea.
Lottery Ticket	7 6	3 6	2 0	1 0
The Clipper of the Clouds	7 6	3 6	2 0	1 0
North against South	7 6	3 6		
Adrift in the Pacific	6 0	3 6		
The Flight to France	7 6	3 6		
The Purchase of the North Pole	6 0			
A Family without a Name	6 0			
Cesar Cascabel	6 0			

Celebrated Travels and Travellers. 3 vols. 8vo, 600 pp., 100 full-page illustrations, 7s. gilt edges, 9s. each:—(1) The Exploration of the World. (2) The Great Navigators of Eighteenth Century. (3) The Great Explorers of the Nineteenth Century.

PERIODICAL PUBLICATIONS

OF

Sampson Low, Marston & Company,

SCRIBNER'S MAGAZINE.

A Superb Illustrated Monthly.   Price One Shilling.

Containing Contributions from the pens of many well-known Authors, among whom may be mentioned Thomas Bailey Aldrich, Sir Edwin Arnold, Andrew Lang, Sarah Orne Jewett, H. M. Stanley, Robert Louis Stevenson, R. H. Stoddard, Frank R. Stockton.

THE NINETEENTH CENTURY

A MONTHLY REVIEW.   Edited by JAMES KNOWLES.

Price Half-a-Crown.

Amongst the contributors the following representative names may be mentioned:—Lord Tennyson, the Right Hon. W. E. Gladstone, Cardinal Manning, Mr. J. A. Froude, Mr. Ruskin, Mr. G. A. Watts, R.A., Earl Grey, the Earl of Derby, Lord Acton, Mr. Herbert Spencer, Mr. Frederic Harrison, Mr. Algernon C. Swinburne, Mr. Leslie Stephen, Professor Huxley, Sir Theodore Martin, Sir Edward Hamley, Professor Goldwin Smith, and Sir Samuel Baker.

THE PUBLISHERS' CIRCULAR,

AND

BOOKSELLERS' RECORD OF BRITISH & FOREIGN LITERATURE.

WEEKLY.   Every Saturday.   Price Three-Halfpence.

SUBSCRIPTION.

Inland ... ... Twelve Months (post free)	8s. 6d.
Countries in the Postal Union ... ,, ,, ,,	11s. 0d.

THE FISHING GAZETTE.

A Journal for Anglers.

Edited by R. B. MARSTON, Hon. Treas. of the Fly Fishers' Club.

Published Weekly, price 2d.   Subscription, 10s. 6d. per annum.

The *Gazette* contains every week Twenty folio pages of Original Articles on Angling of every kind. The paper has recently been much enlarged and improved.

"Under the editorship of Mr. R. B. Marston the *Gazette* has attained a high standing."—*Daily News.*   "An excellent paper."—*The World.*

LONDON: SAMPSON LOW, MARSTON & COMPANY, LIMITED,
ST. DUNSTAN'S HOUSE, FETTER LANE, FLEET STREET, E.C.

www.ingramcontent.com/pod-product-compliance
Lightning Source LLC
Chambersburg PA
CBHW032046220426
43664CB00008B/889